General Billy Mitchell

THEY MADE AMERICA

A series of biographies under the editorship of

Cecile Hulse Matschat   Allan Nevins

Carl Carmer   Lewis Paul Todd

(Additional books in this series are being prepared.)

General Billy Mitchell

CHAMPION OF AIR DEFENSE

66548

ROGER BURLINGAME

McGraw-Hill Book Company, Inc.

NEW YORK   TORONTO   LONDON

GENERAL BILLY MITCHELL: *CHAMPION OF AIR DEFENSE*

Library of Congress Catalog Card Number: 52-12689

Preface

GENERAL MITCHELL is still a controversial figure among his compatriots. I have talked with men who bridle at the mere mention of his name. But there are those, too, who, though they admire his gallantry, sincerely believe that he delayed the cause for which he fought by the bluntness of his approaches.

To others—perhaps to the majority of those who recall his career—he has become the sort of god we often make of our heroes: an object of blind worship. To them he was a martyr to his cause; his conviction, they say, by a military tribunal placed an ineradicable stain on the record of the Army. Some have even gone so far in sentimental hyperbole as to refer to his "crucifixion."

I have tried, in this brief story of his life, to find a path between these extremes. To achieve this, my plan has been to present the man first. If such a presentation is full enough and complete enough, then everything he did becomes credible. But unless we can see his acts in terms of the sort of person he was, they appear unreal and he himself becomes a legendary character subject to many interpretations.

Once we have seen the man, we stop asking ourselves what would have happened if he had done something else:

v

if, for example, he had been more tactful, gentle, subtle, or shrewd. Once we have seen him clearly, we know that he could have behaved in no other way. Right or wrong, Billy Mitchell was direct, forceful, persistent, sparing no one's feelings, refusing to compromise or play games of diplomacy or politics. As we recognize these qualities, we see reasons both for his successes and for the antagonisms he aroused. We accept him, then, not as saint or devil, but as a human fact—an exciting, sharp-edged, highly colored, vocal, intrepid, and often exasperating fact, to be sure, but one about which there can be no "ifs."

I believe Mitchell occupies an important place in our history as the American herald of a world revolution. With that revolution, war and transport moved into a new dimension. Mitchell not only saw it coming; he advanced it in ways which are recognized abroad as well as in America. He practiced concerted attack with large formations of aircraft at a time when military aviation was generally supposed to be concerned only with observation or the direction of artillery fire; in the same era he advocated and demonstrated strategic bombing. He foresaw nearly the air world we live in today with huge planes following the meridians over the Pole to their remote destinations: the ranges and the speeds we know were in his vision. And he saw aircraft out in front of navies as the first line of defense.

His insistent purpose was to keep his country in the van of the change and to make it safe in the new defense terms. He had watched it fall far behind. The battle was less than half-won when he left us. Yet I think he saw victory secure in the years ahead.

In the preparation of this book, I have had generous
help from many quarters. I owe my greatest debt to Mrs.
Thomas Bolling Byrd, General Mitchell's devoted wife
from 1923 to his death in 1936, who gave me permission
to examine the General William Mitchell Papers which
she and her children gave to the Library of Congress in
1949. In addition to this Mrs. Byrd has given me abundant
personal material and has taken me through the Middleburg country in Virginia where she and the general lived
after his resignation from the Army. I am grateful, too, to
Mrs. Kenneth N. Gilpin, Jr., (Lucy Mitchell) and to William Mitchell, Jr., for their assistance and encouragement
and to the general's sister, Mrs. Martin Fladoes (Harriet
Mitchell), who has sent me letters and other material.

My thanks go to Generals Carl Spaatz and Thomas De-
Witt Milling for personal interviews and to General Spaatz
for permission to examine a portion of his collection of papers in the Library of Congress. I have had helpful correspondence with General Frank P. Lahm, who was Chief
of Air Service, Second Army, AEF. Mr. Marvin McFar-
land, of the Aeronautics Division of the Library of Congress, has been of constant assistance, and I also thank
Mr. Arthur G. Renstrom of that department. As he has
done many times before, my friend Mr. David Mearns
simplified my task at the Library of Congress, and Colonel
Willard Webb also helped me there. I wish to thank also
those of the staffs of the Yale University Library and the
New York Public Library who assisted my research.

An eyewitness account of the ship bombing in 1921 was
given me by my friend Thomas Robins. Personal remi-
niscences of General Mitchell were given me by Messrs.

Edward Steichen, John Farrar, Kenneth Littauer, and Gilmore D. Clarke.

In my notes at the end of the book I have given specific sources in printed and manuscript material, but I must mention here the extensive and accurate biography by Isaac Don Levine, *Mitchell: Pioneer of Air Power,* Duell, Sloan & Pearce, Inc., New York, 1943, which anyone who writes about the general must find helpful.

ROGER BURLINGAME

Contents

1

Sunk in a
Hundred Fathoms

THE OCEAN STAGE was set for high drama. Against a backdrop of green sea and steel-blue sky stood the long line of ships of the Atlantic Fleet anchored in 100 fathoms. In the noon calm of a midsummer day they seemed painted there, two-dimensional, silhouettes. To most of the audience packed aboard the transport *Henderson,* the ships stood for reality: solid, enduring facts of defense. In the middle, so rugged that some said it looked like a reef thrust up from the ocean bottom, stood the show's chief prop and symbol. It was a battleship, war-weathered, dirt-gray, squat, ugly, but invincible still—still "dreadnought."

The Germans had called her *Ostfriesland,* "East Frisia." She had survived eighteen hits from 12- and 14-inch guns in the Battle of Jutland in 1916; in her final retreat from that encounter she had struck a mine laid in her path by a British destroyer, yet she had limped home under her own steam. Her triple hull, her eighty-five watertight compartments, her hardened steel armor made her 27,000 tons, in the opinion of naval experts, unsinkable.

1

Yet she had to be sunk. The treaty with the Germans said so. The coalition of Allied Powers, backing international law, could not allow her to be reconditioned and added to the naval strength of the United States. It was a complex business, this international law that condemned a product of years of thought, labor, and technical skill—forty million dollars' worth of forged and tempered steel, delicate machinery, subtle electrical networks—to be sunk in 50 fathoms. But the lawyers who dealt with war thought it just. It kept a balance of power that was supposed to achieve world peace.

The sinking of this unsinkable ship had become immediate necessity. President Wilson's agreement specified the deadline: Sunday, July 24, 1921. It was now high noon on Thursday, July 21. The flagship of the American Atlantic Fleet, the *Pennsylvania,* stood ready with her 14-inch guns to batter the *Ostfriesland* to pieces after the bombs failed. There were those who doubted that even the *Pennsylvania* could do the job. Probably the Navy would have to put demolition explosives inside her hull, place enormous depth bombs under it. In any case it would be fun for the Navy to prove its power. If a battleship were sunk by another battleship, there would be no red faces among naval officers. That was what a queen of the seas was for: to come to grips with another queen. If there was failure, the invincibility of all queens would be proved and the Navy would have to resort to other devices. But the Navy would do it, in the end, not the Army. Above all it would not be done by these frail creatures of the air, these new contraptions, which fanatic visionaries called the "weapons of the future," that had been buzzing this morning and yesterday over the *Ostfriesland* like mosquitoes, as someone said, trying to kill a hippopotamus.

Yet the show had to be played through with the Army, not the Navy, playing the lead. It had to be played this way because the Congress of the United States said so. The jealous armed forces, that knew their places in war so well, were forever being interfered with by this "ignorant" political instrument of the democracy they were supposed to defend. Yet even the untutored landlubbers of Congress would not have fallen for this trick comedy but for the insistent, stubborn prodding of a fanatic brigadier general whom even the Army doubted. He had called in the press to help him, stepped out of the traditional, close-lipped dignity that twenty-three years of service had imposed upon him to rally the people to his side. The Army, surely—though it would be its show—had given him only the weakest support. For, after all, when the curtain came down today and the *Pennsylvania* closed in for the kill, the last laugh would be laughed by the Navy. Yet Congress had said the show must go on; it had appropriated the money. And when the people speaks through its representatives in a nation where the people is sovereign, the word is final.

The audience on the *Henderson*—Army and Navy officers, diplomats, Cabinet members, Senators, Representatives, military and naval attachés of foreign nations, and ubiquitous, cynical newspaper reporters—all these men, had seen this headstrong general. His little two-seater airplane, with its long pennant streaming behind, had circled the *Henderson* more than once in the first acts of the show. Before their eyes the formation of planes he led—they were just beginning to be called "bombers"—had sunk the former German destroyer G-102. Three days ago, when the beautiful 5,000-ton cruiser *Frankfurt* had gone under the waves after army planes had dropped 600-pound bombs on her, the cocky brigadier had flown so low over the *Henderson* that observers on the bridge had ducked their heads. They had seen his face plainly—his flashing eyes, his long nose, his triumphant grin. "Vain," they called him, "braggadocio," "a bundle of conceit," "sensationalist," "headline hunter." Why he wouldn't even wear a regulation army uniform! Some of them had seen him swaggering about Langley Field in an extra-long blouse with flaring pockets like the British, brandishing a gold-headed cane.

There were others, however, aboard the *Henderson* that day who remembered other things about him. He was the first American airman in France in April, 1917—almost before the sound of Wilson's declaration of war had faded in the Capitol; the first American officer to fly over German lines. He had come to command 1,500 "crates" of three nationalities; he had organized the flying wedge that disrupted the base of the German salient at St. Mihiel. He had, a month before the armistice, proposed to General Pershing the unheard-of operation of dropping armed troops by parachute into the enemy's rear. This was pure fancy, of course. Yet it showed an imagination that was rare in the Army. Less imaginary and more stirring to the civilian body of the people had been this general's outcry against the "flaming coffins" which had flown so many young American pilots to their death.

Opinion aboard the *Henderson* was split. It was the kind of spirit that has always occurred in the great moments of world change. On one side stood the adherents to tradition, who clung to the principles that had brought the glories of the past. They were the "Rock of Gibraltar" people. They believed in solid bulwarks of defense. They kept their faith in the impregnable. Their minds were like those of the strategists who at that moment were planning the Maginot line in France, a string of fortresses that no force of men and guns could batter down. They loved the *status quo* and clung to it. And was there ever a symbol of the *status quo* like the battleship?

On the other side stood those whose belief in any *status quo* had been shattered by a machine that flew through the air at 100 miles an hour and was carrying men to new and ever-changing destinies. What price any fortress that was anchored to the earth when man could leapfrog over it? What price size, bulk, solidity, thickness as road blocks in the path of the eagle? No, the world of the future was to be a world, not of static matter, but of speed, altitude, incessant motion. Whether today a David of the air would slay a Goliath of the sea with a 2,000-pound slingshot did not greatly matter: he would do it tomorrow or the day after—next month, next year. It was in the cards; it was in the stars, and you gray-headed, gold-braided admirals had better make up your minds to it and stop weeping over the nobility, the grandeur, and the queenly power of forty million dollars' worth of junk!

The arguments were still hot, and bets were mounting as eight bells struck on the *Henderson*.

"Nothing that's happened so far proves anything."

"All the same, she's down a little by the stern. Since yesterday's bombing."

"Last night she listed to starboard. This morning she's righted herself."

"Listen to this—about yesterday—in *The New York Times:* 'Altogether it was a great day for advocates of the battleship and a poor one for those who have been contending that battleships will be at the mercy of bombing airmen from the coast.'"

"Wait a minute. That story is about 600-pounders. He's using 2,000-pounders today."

"That's impossible. No plane can carry a ton of bomb."

"Ask the general——"

General Williams, Chief of Ordnance, nodded confirmation. The bombs, he said, were the largest ever made. They had been delivered to Langley Field just in time. The Ordnance people had been afraid they wouldn't make it. In hot weather it takes ten days or more for TNT to cool after it is poured. Suddenly one of the bright boys in the department had had a brain storm and packed the bombs in ice. Yes, they were there all right.

"It's one thing to have them at Langley Field and another to fly them 80 miles to sea in a flimsy aircraft."

A reporter spoke. "I've just been up on the bridge," he said, "talking to Glenn Martin. He says his ships have been tested with dummies. His bombers are new, different from anything we've seen. Two engines——"

"He ought to know."

"Whatever happens, it won't prove anything. Look at the target—a sitting duck. In wartime she would be under steam, moving."

"If she were moving, she would be easier to hit from

the air. The ratio of speeds would be less. What's more, in wartime her magazines would be filled. A direct hit would detonate them."

"I understand he isn't going to try for direct hits. He's working with the water hammer."

"What?"

"Remember, when we were kids, we clicked stones together under water and the noise almost broke our eardrums? That proves the terrific effect of submarine explosions. Direct hits didn't sink the *Frankfurt*. Bombs in the water off her bows opened the seams. The reason that battleship out there listed last night was because the 600-pounders yesterday landed in the water too near her."

So the talk went. Engineers, distinguished professors of physics, and aircraft designers told their stories, and naval officers shook their heads. They were practical men who knew the sea. But they were curiously emotional men, too, some of them, about ships. The commander of a ship loves her—often more than he loves his wife. If she sinks, he expects to go down with her. There is, perhaps, no more dominating, sentimental attachment in the armed forces of the world. Through history it has been the undercurrent of battles and storms, of high nights in the wardroom, the silent accompaniment of toasts to king and admiral.

Since these men had seen only white swirling water where the *Frankfurt* had floated a scant twenty minutes before, they had been vaguely uneasy. The *Frankfurt* was only a cruiser, after all, and a small one built for speed not resistance. Yet she was a handsome vessel, and most of the watchers from the Navy had commanded such a one. It was rumored that even "he," himself, the upstart air general, had hated to see her sink—an Army man with no sentiment at all.

But since the *Frankfurt* there had been betrayal within the circle of the Navy itself. Nothing more had been heard of Secretary Daniels's earlier offer to stand on the bridge of a ship while she was being bombed by aircraft. And the celebrated Admiral Sims had said publicly that battleships were obsolete, and his words were echoed by Admiral Fullam. Both these hoary sailors were retired, of course, and probably in their second childhood. Yet their irresponsible words must have made the great Mahan, who had laid down eternal laws in his *Sea Power*, turn in his grave. New "science," these old men had said, was nullifying the laws. The hell with "science"! It was ruining war. So the naval men had turned away from the physicists, leaned on the rail, brought their glasses to rest on the German dreadnought. Thus, for the moment, their confidence returned.

It was then, when the reporters had scribbled their notes on the conversations and the smiling Japanese naval attaché had buttoned away his secret memorandums, that the word came down from the crow's-nest and moved rapidly forward and aft along the decks of the *Henderson*. "They" had been sighted on the western horizon. There was a rush for the vantage points that was almost too hurried for the important dignity of the audience. On the bridge, admirals held gold chronometer watches in their hands and searched the sky with glasses. When they had spotted the aircraft, they glanced back at the anchored airplane tender *Shawmut,* from which the tests were to be directed by signal and radio. On the *Shawmut* were the officials from the Navy to see that the Navy's strict rules were obeyed. The Navy, after all, was running the show. The Navy had laid down rules that were tough. Some said they were too tough, that no airman could follow them and do a proper job. It was rumored that they had demanded an altitude too high for bomb-laden airplanes. They could stop the bombing at any time by belching black smoke from the *Shawmut*'s funnel. They had stopped it that way this morning—no one seemed to know why—and the little planes had flown back to Langley for more gas. Gas was a crucial business in 1921.

Backers of the airmen said the Navy did not want them to succeed; that the direction of the show was especially designed to delay the bombing until the gas gave out. The Navy had provided rescue apparatus to prevent serious casualties if the gas did give out or if squalls or mechanical failures brought the frail aircraft down. Blimps hovered overhead ready to descend and pick up victims of ditching. Fast little tenders were ready to help. And there was a hospital ship. The admirals looked these things over with satisfaction. They could not hear the laughter of the pilots above them.

It did not take long for the specks on the horizon to become airplanes directly overhead. Yet even at 1,700 feet their size was not impressive. Experts spotted a Handley-Page and six Martin bombers as they passed above the *Henderson.* They were climbing then, and by the time they were over the target, they were harder to distinguish. The chronometers' hands touched 12:17. The airplanes circled, climbed, and formed far apart in a long, straight line.

There was sudden laughter on the *Henderson*. The first Martin had passed over the *Ostfriesland*, and there was a tiny splash in the water. Someone shouted angrily, "It's a ranging shot, you fools, a 25-pounder." Then a yell went up from the decks.

"There he is! The pennant! Look!"

And there he was, sure enough, too high now for them to see his grin, climbing over the target till he was almost invisible. Below him the second Martin came over the battleship. From her belly fell something no one had seen before. It was long, thin, cigar-shaped. It seemed to fall slowly, tumbling over and over, catching the sunlight as it turned. From the sea came a splash followed by a column of black-and-white smoke shooting hundreds of feet in the air. And then rose a column of water. As it broke, high above the battleship, the *Henderson* trembled through its length and the men on the decks reached for the rail and the stanchions. Then the water fell over the *Ostfriesland;* it covered the whole of her hull, so that only her masts and funnels showed. The roar of the explosion was still echoing when the next Martin came over.

The 2,000-pound bombs fell from the Martins almost exactly two minutes apart. As the smoke cleared after each, the *Ostfriesland* was still gallantly floating. The watchers on the *Henderson* could see no wounds. The naval officers slapped one another on the back. "See! They can't sink her!" But when the last Martin had dropped its bellyful, the water did not clear from the *Ostfriesland's* afterdeck. Then slowly she listed to port. The motion was infinitely slow, like the movements of a great sea monster whose brain has just become aware of mortal hurt. As, with the same slow turn and lift, the bow came up, the men on the *Henderson* stopped talking. The only sound came from the drone of the Martins circling overhead. No one spoke even when the enormous gaping holes in the hull under the bow came into view; or when a little airplane with a long pennant streaming out behind shot down until it almost touched the tilted masts and rose again. No one took his eyes from his glasses. No one laughed or cheered.

Here and there an officer—or a reporter—stood with a watch and a notebook jotting down minutes and seconds. At 12:33 P.M. the *Ostfriesland's* stern was under water. Four minutes later she rolled over completely. At 12:38 P.M. she was almost perpendicular, her bow in the air, one mast and three funnels under. She stood so for two minutes that seemed an hour without moving, as if her stern rested on the bottom. Then the bow went under all at once, and there was nothing but a circle of white water. It was then that the Handley-Page, which everyone had forgotten, dropped from high in the sky and her bomb fell in the center of the circle.

An old officer put his arms on the rail and his head in his arms and wept.

Up and down the decks trite, meaningless words were uttered abruptly by men too deeply stirred to order their thoughts. It was a release when the cheer came from everywhere at once. It is good to yell when you cannot speak; even when you are yelling at a small two-seater airplane with a pennant and when you feel quite sure that the long-nosed, smiling, helmeted pilot cannot hear you above the sound of his engine.

The cheer was partly for a new world in the air when the old one had just sunk into the sea. And it was partly—mostly—for General Billy Mitchell.

2

A Wisconsin Dynasty

HE WAS BORN in Nice, on the Mediterranean coast of France, in a time of great peace in the world. There was good will among nations. Nearly ten years had healed the wounds inflicted in the last sizable war in 1870. A wise queen sat on the English throne, and her ministers believed that diplomacy, rather than war, was the right answer to international arguments. It was true, to be sure, that the most powerful navy the world had even seen stood behind this policy. But it was also true that this indestructible, "unsinkable" navy was used as an instrument of peace as a thoughtfully directed police force is used for the safety of citizens.

It was possible to travel in 1879 without passports. Americans moved freely all over Europe. And the gates of the United States were open to the world. In the West of America there still seemed to be endless opportunity for everyone—for prosperity if not for riches. In the American East new marvels of science or invention were constantly appearing. The 1870s had already produced the telephone, the phonograph, the typewriter, quantity production of steel, and spectacular railroad development.

The era seems, in contrast to the warring years in which this boy came to know both triumph and disaster, a time of busy progress in world harmony. Whatever forces were already at work to throw civilization into chaos were not apparent unless one looked with prophetic eyes into the German, Austro-Hungarian, and Russian empires. From the French Riviera, where John Lendrum Mitchell and his bride of a year were enjoying the warm winter sunshine, such forces were far away.

William arrived—a belated Christmas present and almost a New Year's gift to his parents—on December 29. That he should arrive in Nice rather than in Milwaukee did not disturb the Mitchells, although his father took immediate care to register him as an American. John Mitchell had been educated in Europe and loved the Old World as he loved his native Wisconsin, but for different reasons. The ancient traditions were a balance to the pioneer freshness. His blood had been nourished by the soil of the West; his mind by the history, the philosophies, the literature, and the languages of Europe. It was an uncommon thing for Milwaukee citizens of that day to live so much so far from home. But the Mitchells had earned leisure. John's father, Alexander, was too busy creating a state and a city to leave them. That was why, no doubt, he used a part of the fortune that he had won in the wild lands to bring his son in touch with an older civilization. These facts—the wealth and the foreign culture—were to have a profound influence on the robust baby in Nice. The spoon that was in the baby's mouth at his birth was of solid gold—not plated with gilt like the spoons of so many children of the American rich.

When William began to talk, he was bilingual: the French was said to be better than the English. The French was teased out of him after he came home and began going to school in Milwaukee. The children of the pioneers could not take it. Willie forgot it—deliberately and angrily—until, nearly forty years later, it became part of his job. Like many foreign-born Americans he became, in Milwaukee, passionately American—too violently patriotic sometimes for his father's comfort. Yet the influence was still there: the map in the child's mind stretched far beyond America until at last it rounded into a globe.

The Mitchell family had long been leaders in Milwaukee when Willie arrived there from France in 1883. The principal reason for this was neither Alexander's wealth nor John's education. It was because Alexander, coming from Scotland to the little lake-shore village in 1839, had established a banking institution in which the whole of the West had faith. There was little money in those days of wildcat finance. Goods were bought with other goods, and property was bought with IOUs. These promissory notes were good only if you knew the man who gave them; the paper money became worthless a few miles away from its place of issue. Nothing stood behind it but a man's blind faith in tomorrow. Tomorrow in those tremendous times of expansion and building was likely to be golden, but many people were intent on getting there first and the devil take the hindmost. Scores of crooks were scattered through the ranks of the brave pioneers.

Nothing whatever stood behind the bank notes printed by Alexander Mitchell and his associate George Smith except Alexander Mitchell and George Smith. Yet such was the honesty and good faith of these gentlemen—especially Mitchell after Smith retired—that "Mitchell money" came to be accepted all the way from the Alleghenies to the Mississippi and beyond. It built Milwaukee. It even reached out to help build Chicago. It is no wonder then that, in their prosperity of the 1880s, the people were grateful to the old Scot.

Alexander Mitchell was a true Scot. He always kept some of his money laid aside for a rainy day. And rainy days came every so often, even in the land of endless opportunity. There was a real cloudburst, for instance, in 1873 in the form of a panic. It swept the savings of millions down the drain. The Civil War, the reckless postwar spending, the operations of "robber barons," orgies of swindling, the extravagance of railroad builders had made it look as if the inexhaustible wealth had been exhausted. Actually all the panic had done was to build a wall between wealth and money. The wealth was still there and Alexander Mitchell knew it. He threw in his fair-weather savings and kept his bank going when the banks of the country were falling like houses of cards.

Son John differed from the old man, believing that money should be enjoyed. He bought Meadowmere, a 400-acre estate complete with woods and pasture, and made on it lakes and a private racecourse. He used the land for all it was worth. He bred cattle and race horses on a large scale, and it never struck him as odd for a scholar to engage in such a business. John Mitchell always used to the full the opportunities offered by the place where he was. He was as absorbed by the Wisconsin soil as by the European culture.

Willie, as his family called him, grew up on this estate in Milwaukee County. Meadowmere was paradise to an active boy. Willie was so active that there was not a moment left for undirected thought. His ambition to perfect himself in every conceivable strength and skill of body seemed to his friends like mania. He rode every intractable horse till he mastered it; he became an indefatigable and fast swimmer; before his teens he was expert with shotgun and rifle. As well as shooting birds, he studied their habits, learned to stuff them, and collected them until he was able to present the Milwaukee Museum with a collection of which it has ever since been proud. When once he had determined to learn something, he learned it thoroughly: nothing would keep him from constant practice and study until he was expert in every detail. As he learned to handle a horse or gun, so he eventually learned Spanish, telegraphy, scouting, managing dog sleds, commanding troops, and, at last, flying.

He was apt, to be sure, having a strong body, automatic coordination, and a quick mind. His family was a help to him. His mother was fearless and wanted her boy to grow up unafraid. Once, when he told her he could not ride a certain horse, she said, "Keep on riding him till you can." His father had learned discipline in the Army in the Civil War, and when Willie was cantankerous—as he must often have been—the chances are that punishment was swift. John Mitchell had no expectation or desire in those days that Willie should become a soldier. John Mitchell hated war. But he knew that a normal boy is happier under discipline than without it.

But neither Meadowmere nor his family was wholly responsible for Willie's habits. The fact was that he was entirely concerned with things outside himself. When psychologists began to call people names according to their behavior, they called Willie's kind "extrovert." He was concerned with things rather than thoughts. His concentration on work or sport was never interrupted by doubts about his performance. He never stopped to ask himself, "How am I doing?" or "What are people thinking of me?" He did not go into long periods of daydreaming in which he doubted whether he was fit for this or that or felt shame for something he had done or self-consciousness about his appearance; whether or not he was in love or worthy of his love's object. Unlike his father, he did not speculate about God, immortality, the universe, economic theories, or social ideals. He accepted God without argument as he accepted the flag, the Constitution, America's "manifest destiny," and, when it arrived, love. He accepted the universe as exceedingly interesting without worrying about where it came from.

Underneath all this was a solid core of self-confidence. He knew precisely his own capacities—he had tried them out and proved them—so there was no need to speculate. He did not say, "I wonder if I can do this"; he tried it. He was certain, once he had accepted a belief, that he was right. This certainly made enemies. He was called "vain," "arrogant," "stuck up"; it was said he had a closed mind. None of these things was true in the ordinary sense, for these qualities are ordinarily accompanied by hypocrisy or bluff. Billy Mitchell, even when he was Willie Mitchell, was sincere: there was nothing of the "four-flusher" about him.

We see in the lad at Meadowmere good material for the Army. He probably learned about the Army from his friend and neighbor Douglas MacArthur. Douglas's father, Arthur, was a colonel in those days and away from home for long periods of time. His boys, Arthur and Douglas, were destined for the armed forces: Arthur was aiming for Annapolis, Douglas for West Point. But young Mitchell did not stay at home long enough for the MacArthur influence to become binding upon him. He was sent to school at Racine, then to college at George Washington University. When he met the Army again, it was on its way to war.

3

Call to Arms

IT IS HARD, looking back across all the bloody battlefields
of later conflicts to 1898 and the Spanish-American War,
to understand how anyone could have taken it seriously.
To young men of today, to their parents, to statesmen and
Presidents, war is an unhappy business, necessary to survival, made necessary by the conspiracies of evil men.
Flag waving, martial music, bugle calls, and uniforms have
lost their glamor. Incendiary speeches in Congress are
heard with cynical apathy. Rabble-rousing propaganda
may stir the youth of Moscow, but it can no longer persuade the boys of New York, San Francisco, Chicago, New
Orleans, or Milwaukee that they are about to engage in a
"crusade." It is difficult, therefore, to put ourselves in the
place of Billy Mitchell as he stood in the gallery of the
Senate in April, 1898, and heard the "call to arms" against
a feeble and reluctant power which had been turned into
an enemy by mass meetings, eagle-screaming oratory, and
the all-time low in yellow journalism.

But to Billy Mitchell, just past his eighteenth birthday,
war was adventure. His generation—in the North, at least
—had been brought up on tales of the Civil War which

emphasized heroism above horror. In their lifetime no gun had been fired except in salute. War was a proud uniform brought out of camphor balls for an annual parade; it was "Marching through Georgia" played by a fife-and-drum corps; it was a mystery story of valiant spies behind an enemy's lines, a tale of urgent dispatches borne by a galloping horseman through rains of fire which always missed, of the raising of Old Glory above a battered fort. The men who told these yarns to their young omitted the boredom of waiting for contact, the disease of the camps, the gangrene on the field, the vermin in the prisons; the sacrifices, the grief, the profiteering, and the subtle treasons on the home front. Or, if they told these, too, the young exercised their powers of selective deafness.

To Billy Mitchell the resounding declaration on Capitol Hill opened a vista of opportunity for the exploiting of all his perfected skills. Strength of muscle, bodily endurance, sure fire with every sort of small arm, accomplished horsemanship, understanding of terrain, a flair for quick decision, and that habit of prophetic thinking so peculiarly his —of always figuring on the next move—where but in a fighting army could such a combination of talents find full scope? As usual Billy Mitchell wasted no time speculating, wondering, or doubting. He had no responsibilities. His formal education was nearly completed. He had no plans for a career which war would interrupt. He walked directly from the Capitol to his father and announced his decision to enlist immediately.

John Mitchell had by this time become a United States Senator. He had moved into temporary residence on the Hill (where the Senate office building now stands), so

Billy had only a few hundred yards to walk. Accustomed as he must have been to these flash decisions, the Senator was disturbed by his son's announcement. He had counted on Billy's graduation from George Washington University. Yet he had himself met war on the threshold of college, and he had come to accept it as the tragic result of "cosmic" trends, against which individual dissenting men could do little. In the Senate he began by opposing the trend toward armed intervention in Cuba, but after an American battleship had exploded and sunk in Havana Harbor, he knew that uninformed American opinion had become a tidal wave, and he had voted in the end for war.

Now before him stood, not a little boy valiantly sweating to avoid defeat by physical forces, but a full-grown, strong-willed, sound-bodied man, most of whose weaknesses and failures were behind him. The discipline that had made this son's character was no longer applicable against him. John Mitchell could not continue to look out of his philosophical ivory tower into those determined eyes. He could almost hear the echo of the martial music in his son's mental ears. Turning away from this astonishing adult spectacle which seemed to have appeared overnight, he passed the buck to Billy's mother. "With her consent you may go."

Harriet Becker Mitchell was a realist. In eighteen years six other children had followed Billy. She knew there was no longer any place for her first-born in the nest. He had grown strong enough to fly as far as he wished from home, and she recognized the wish quickly. The question of consent was an academic one. She gave it without argument, formally, with neither a sigh nor a wink at the inexorable Fate with which she was conniving. Nor was there, in all probability, any later family discussion while Billy was on the night train to Milwaukee. Harriet Mitchell knew that her son was cast trait for trait in her own mold: that, when she faced him on that April day, Greek was meeting Greek and that quick compliance was easier than slow defeat.

From the blare of trumpets in April to the humiliating treaty in December, the war with Spain seems to our hardened eyes to have been a wholly amateur performance. There was no thought of a draft. The volunteers were organized locally into outfits of the state militia. Naïvely these home-town regiments elected their own officers on a basis of local popularity. Young Mitchell, in the First Wisconsin, which seems to have had some vague traditional glamor dating from the 1860s, was instantly aware of his own officers' ineptitude for military ventures, their total ignorance of organization, logistics, operations, intelligence, or even the most primitive rules of camp sanitation. In the Milwaukee camp, patriotism and snappy performance of the manual of arms were more important than cots, insect screens, sequestered latrines, pure water supply, or inspected rations, and in a matter of weeks disease more than decimated the roster. This, of course, was only a foretaste of what was to come in tropical climates, but it may have toughened some of the survivors. None of this dampened young Mitchell's ardor while his iron constitution kept him healthy, but it may have sowed those seeds of discontent with military inefficiency which years later were to produce such bitter fruit.

These conditions were not confined to Milwaukee. They were true throughout the country. Military camps were crowded with the families of soldiers and every other sort of camp follower, who brought quantities of indigestible food to give or sell to the heroes and demoralize discipline. The whole mobilization had the look of a round of parties. Frederick Funston reports the appearance at inspection of soldiers with bouquets from last night's dance tucked in their web belts. At the frequent parades civilian patriots expressed their fervor by throwing firecrackers at the horses. Casualties were already high before the regiments were transferred to embarkation points by delayed trains moving under mixed orders, but in the new camps in hot Florida they were increased by spoiled food and fever-bearing mosquitoes.

The First Wisconsin was still in Milwaukee when news came like a thunderbolt which changed the whole aspect of the war. Overnight the eyes of the American people were forced to shift from Cuba in the Caribbean, where an American army was expected to strike the shackles of oppression from suffering Cubans, to the Philippine Islands some 800 miles off the coast of Southeast Asia. Millions of geographies were opened that startled morning in an effort to find the whereabouts of a place called Manila, and from that moment the curtain came down on American isolation.

In those preradio days news came first on bulletin boards outside the city newspaper offices; later in the semifictional "extra" editions of the papers, which made quick and extraordinary profits for the publishers. In our time, with radio, television, and all the news services at work, the kind of lying that was easy for "scooping" journalism in the 1890s has become impossible. There was no check then on rumor: sensational stories had to be printed quickly and at length, so imaginative talent was essential to profit. No publisher today can boast, as William Randolph Hearst did in 1898, that he is "making" a war. This power of the press, which on the first day of May, 1898, persuaded the American people, who had gone to bed in a republic, to accept an empire with their breakfast coffee, cannot be ignored in any study of this astonishing era.

The bulletins said Commodore George Dewey had sailed his fleet flagship the *Olympia* into Manila Bay in the Philippine Islands. The papers, on our streets an hour later, gave the assurance that the American flag waved over the entire Philippine archipelago. Actually the only communiqués which had come in were enemy reports sent from Madrid. Not a whisper had crossed the Pacific. Except for the fact that alarmed Spaniards in their home capital were telling of attack on their Pacific colony plus the fact that the United States Navy Department had issued Dewey's orders, nothing was known. Actually it was three months later that Manila was occupied by American marines—an event which precipitated a new war and opened, for Billy Mitchell, a second glamorous vista—but by that time the people had fully accepted and celebrated the fact of world power for their nation. Forty-four years later, when Mitchell's playmate Douglas MacArthur stood with his back to the Corregidor wall, they were still accepting it but with less certainty; fifty-three years later, when the same MacArthur was grimly clinging to Pusan, they were accepting it with misgivings and occasional regret.

Mitchell, while all this was happening, was still in the fly-ridden discomfort of the Milwaukee camp. He may have been less impressed at the moment by Dewey's triumph than disturbed by the fear that the war in Cuba might be over before he got into it. He was already a soldier among awkward civilians. His appearance in the regiment on parade was already that of a professional. In spite of his age he was obvious officer material. He probably contributed much to a morale which sweat, sickness, and waiting were beginning to dissolve. He accepted every dirty detail with the cheerful conviction that it was an essential part of a glorious whole.

His regiment went to Florida in May, and immediately afterward an unexpected thing happened. There entered, at this point in Billy Mitchell's career, a person destined to have a long, deep influence upon it. Perhaps he did not know, when the thing happened in Florida, that Brigadier General Adolphus Washington Greely was responsible. What happened was a special order that Private Mitchell proceed at once to Washington to receive an officer's commission.

General Greely after a celebrated career as an Arctic explorer—in which he had almost lost his life—had become Chief Signal Officer of the United States Army. The Signal Corps in those days was a minor department. Just before the declaration of war it comprised a total of five officers, eighty sergeants, and three thousand dollars. These were supposed to cover field communications by telegraph, telephone, wigwag, photography, and observation balloons. As Mitchell later wrote, the conservative officers of the line of the Army actually believed, as late as the 1890s, that a galloping messenger was a better means of communication than any electrical device! So, until Greely took charge and fought such superstitions, a dim view of the Signal Corps was held by some of the most gallant graduates of West Point.

A tall, robust, and rugged man with a large, handsomely cut black beard, General Greely had a scientific mind in tune with the best prophets of the time who saw a new world beyond the horizon. Was it coincidence or one of those uncanny designs of Fate that he was a close friend of the Mitchells, of Milwaukee: that he had watched the growing up of a boy in Meadowmere and had recognized a kindred mind?

In any case, when Billy arrived in Washington, protesting at orders which removed him from an outfit he liked, he found himself a second lieutenant in the Signal Corps and, after brief communication with the chief, he quickly guessed why. Soon after he arrived, accident or destiny threw in his way a chance to distinguish himself. Seventy-five New York volunteers, passing through Washington on their way to the war, deserted their train and went AWOL en masse. Their officers, separated from them by the current "social register" custom, had gone on in their Pullmans blissfully unaware that they had lost their command. The soldiers, ill-fed and neglected, stormed into the street and captured a hotel after subduing the proprietor, the staff, and particularly the bartender. They then treated themselves to the privileges of free guests.

There being no MP in those days, the helpless city police called the War Department, and it sent a riot call to Billy Mitchell's barracks. He instantly scented adventure and asked to go to the hotel's rescue. He took fourteen men, commandeered a trolley car, and arrived quickly at the scene of the disturbance.

From inside the hotel came shouts and singing. The proprietor, wringing his hands, told Billy that "the soldiers were all drunk and very dangerous, and that anybody who went in would probably be killed." The proprietor was alarmed, no doubt, at discovering that his rescue was in the hands of an eighteen-year-old boy and not an unusually big one at that.

Billy had with him, however, two "enormous" men. He put them at the two exits, gave them orders to unload and use only their rifle butts, distributed the others at strategic points outside, and went with one man into the bar. He found the seventy-five soldiers in precisely the condition the proprietor had described. Several of them were mixing drinks behind the bar. The others were singing, yelling, and throwing bottles at the plate-glass mirror.

According to his own account, Billy was so amused at this sight that he could hardly control his voice. He did, however, and called the one command which soldiers obey even in their sleep. The word was "Attention!" He had been an officer a matter of days; yet he knew the power of the word. Seventy-two soldiers rose and clicked their heels. The other three could not rise.

With a sequence of other sharp orders he got the men in formation. He then marched them 3 miles. On the way he detached men to fill buckets from the hydrants they passed to pour over those who were still semiconscious. At the end of this forced march all the men were sober and sorry.

General Greely read with eagerness his new lieutenant's report of the venture. Like all good generals, Greely was careful in his comment. He told Mitchell his report was "short, concise, to the point and understandable" in spite, he added, of its remarkable spelling and punctuation, which Billy would do well to watch in the future. But the general must have been privately impressed by an eighteen-year-old's restraint in acting unarmed, his complete self-confidence in meeting this mob with only one assistant, and especially by his knowledge of the psychological effect of an officer's power of presence and voice in a crisis. It was, perhaps, this single episode which kept the general's interest in Mitchell's military powers, and it was their later community of interest that led Mitchell into the sky.

The stay at Washington Barracks was temporary, and Billy was soon on his way to Florida, this time with the Signal Corps.

The camp to which he was assigned in Jacksonville suffered through the hot summer. But Mitchell never fell into the prevailing habit of killing time with poker, checkers, or the endless analysis of "latrine rumor." He learned the Morse code, wigwagging, and telegraphy; he studied from books every detail of field telephony and applied his knowledge with experimental wire. He used the "golden spoon" to buy himself a thoroughbred, and he spent his leaves on hunting expeditions while his colleagues caroused on the eat-drink-and-be-merry formula in Jacksonville.

He never got into combat in the war. The headline triumphs of "Fighting Joe" Wheeler in Daiquirí, Siboney, and Santiago, the dismounted charge of Teddy Roosevelt and his "rough riders" up San Juan Hill, and even the bloodless capture of Havana had all been accomplished before Lieutenant Mitchell left Florida for Cuba. Yet he was glad to get there even in an army of occupation and wrote on Christmas Eve an enthusiastic letter to his father from Quemados, where he sat "on a high bluff overlooking the sea" and thrilled with patriotism because the sky, with sunset and stars, looked "like our flag."

4

Philippine Adventure

CUBA WAS STILL ADVENTURE to Lieutenant Mitchell after the brave dreams of most of the other volunteers had faded into fever and homesickness. That he remained healthy, energetic, and cheerful in the enervating climate with sickness and despair all about him seems miraculous when we read about the shattered morale in the camps of the occupation army.

The army, wrote Major William C. Gorgas, the great American doctor in charge of the hospital at Camp Columbia, "was utterly used up and of no value whatever as a fighting machine. Fully four-fifths of the men were having fever. . . . After the surrender of the Spanish garrison there was a complete let-down on our side. Everybody wanted to go home. . . . Officers and men became nervous and hysterical. . . . Many times every day the poor fellows, officers and men, would break down and cry when told they could not leave on the next ship."

In fact, however, there was no miracle in Mitchell's resistance to disease and doldrums. Nor was it an instance of that blind luck that is thought by his more romantic biographers to have followed him through life, saving him in hundreds of escapades on the threshold of death. There was no factor of luck in these escapes. The factors were training and a complete, subconscious knowledge of what he was doing. When he did not have that certainty, he had "bad luck" aplenty. His mistakes, however, when he made them, did not endanger his life.

Nor did he deserve any particular moral credit for resisting the temptations that beset so many young soldiers in the dismal boredom of postwar Cuba. For him the temptations simply did not exist. The indulgences which abused health did not amuse him. The activities he passionately enjoyed all contributed to his fitness. He was exceedingly proud of that fitness. He wrote home repeatedly that, in the midst of dying men, he had not even "had a cold."

His health was also supported by his mental attitude. He was often restless in times of quiet—itching and scheming to get into hotter activity—yet he was never bored. He never fell into the army habit of doing nothing when there was nothing to do. In lax hours he invented useful occupations. Always these were jobs that would help him in the next move. His greatest talent was his gift for thinking in futures. This is something that must never be forgotten. He had the mind of a great chess player who in the middle of a game sees its end. The trouble was that the board he had to play on was the United States Army, and here, he discovered well on in the game, the squares were irregular, pieces were missing, and the rules were occasionally similar to those Alice met on the other side of the looking glass.

In spare time Mitchell learned Spanish. He studied military history from Caesar to Napoleon. He studied the Cubans and, being able to talk to them, made new judgments. (They were not all, he found, the heroes the newspapers had made of them.) He worked at the geography, flora, fauna, and climate of the island. Then he was given a job into which all this knowledge fitted. The job also fitted his restless, active temperament and kept him continually busy from January to June.

The job was to go out with a detachment of forty men and string approximately 140 miles of telegraph line over the island. He was entirely on his own. For a month he was out of communication with the world. He had to cope not only with the jungle but with the guerrilla bandits which such a war always leaves behind it. His success proved his understanding of tactics, terrain, and the simpler techniques of the telegraph, but most of all it proved his ability to get along with men, the first requirement of a good officer.

By June, when the assignment was completed, he had become a professional. Whether he knew it or not, the Army had set its seal on him. It was not the sort of seal either the Academy or the ranks usually sets upon a man. It had not adapted him to the long, slow routine of a post, to the dullness of close-order drill, to the rigid adherence to a book of regulations, or the red tape of seniority promotion. That sort of patience was not one of Billy Mitchell's virtues, and it was not in his character to conform. But as long as there was a specialty—as there certainly was in the Signal Corps—in which he could use his brains and work independently, the Army would fulfill all his desires.

He was eager, in June, 1899, for combat. In Cuba he had been deprived of that, however much Cuba had prepared him for war somewhere else. In June he knew that the last vestige of war had disappeared from Cuba, but he also knew that there was war elsewhere—a wilderness war, a wild, mountainous, sniping, treacherous war that would take all a man's ingenuity and offer him a chance for individual achievement. With his job done in Cuba, the knowledge gave him the itch of a hair shirt.

Commodore George Dewey had sat in the *Olympia,* anchored off Manila, through the summer of 1898. He had destroyed the Spanish ships in the bay. Yet the city of Manila itself remained in the hands of the enemy, and Dewey had no army with which to take it. The government had sent no army, being assured by the Navy that, the instant their ships were destroyed, the Spaniards would surrender the city. And so indeed they might have done had the situation on the island of Luzon been in their control. The Spaniards reconciled themselves, early in the summer, to losing the war. But a curious and wholly unexpected conflict had arisen.

The government at Washington and the American newspapers had proclaimed that their motive in the Philippines had been the same as that in Cuba: to free the unhappy natives from Spanish oppression. This President McKinley seems to have sincerely believed. Many Senators and Representatives, however, and a large part of the American people, their desire for empire having been whipped up by the press and by the speeches of local patriots, were attached to the idea that the Pacific islands were a fine new colony, rich in natural resources, ripe for exploitation. Even these patriots, to be sure, made ample use in their propaganda of the old formula of the "white man's burden" and many pious words about civilizing and educating the "savages." And behind all this, as always, powerful commercial interests were at work.

The Filipinos had rebelled against Spanish rule much as the Cubans had done. But they had fought for total independence. This, in the declaration of war, the United States had definitely promised the Cubans. It had, however, ignored the Filipinos. On the island of Luzon one exceedingly astute, educated, and intelligent Filipino had remembered this on the day Dewey arrived, and immediately he investigated. He went to Singapore and to Hong Kong and talked to the American consuls there. He also conferred with the consul who had remained in Manila. From none of them could he get the assurance that the Americans were prepared to turn over the Philippine archipelago to its natives the instant Spain ceded it to the United States. He, therefore, proceeded at once to organize a large and powerful army among his compatriots.

Emilio Aguinaldo has come to be regarded as an officer and a gentleman, a civilized and honest patriot—however brutal and treacherous his subordinates may have been. But to Dewey, waiting anxiously on his flagship, Aguinaldo and his insurgent soldiers who, Intelligence reported, were well armed were a greater menace than the Spaniards. Indeed, in one of those queer twists which sometimes occur in the midst of conflict, the Spanish on Luzon suddenly became our friends and tried to help us capture Manila!

Admiral Dewey had already sensed the difficulty in May and cabled home for an army. It arrived by slow steamers in August. It captured Manila on the fourteenth and sat down in the city, where presently it found itself besieged by Aguinaldo's forces. It remained there through the autumn and the winter of 1898 while the treaty of peace was signed with Spain, and in the spring of 1899, while Billy Mitchell was stringing wires across Cuba, the United States was faced with a full-scale war against the people whom presumably it had set out to save.

The United States up to that time had had no foreign policy whatever except the Monroe Doctrine, adequately protected by the British navy. For more than twenty years after the Civil War we had had no navy of our own beyond a few obsolete ships which had been occupied in making "courtesy calls" in the world's ports. In the 1890s all this had changed. Finally splendid isolation had vanished with Dewey's broadsides in Manila Bay, and in a few months the American State Department had to think up a foreign policy covering the vast Pacific without the aid of radio or aviation and with a navy far from adequate in ships and gunnery to enforce its decrees. It is hardly surprising that this first policy was hesitant, vague, and amateurish, but it is almost miraculous that in the half century since we have become leader of the world's powers, successful in two world wars, with the world's largest navy and an air force of the highest potential. It is useful to remember these things in our hours of doubt.

Lieutenant William Mitchell, in his twentieth summer, was less concerned with the ethics of the Philippine war than was his father. Senator Mitchell stood with the anti-imperialist Democrats. He had become reconciled to the war in Cuba, finding justification in the promise of independence. He never accepted the Pacific annexations. He opposed the bloodless attachment of Hawaii and the exceedingly bloody conquest of the Philippines. But Billy, like many of the robust, exuberant youths of his day, was all expansionist; he would have liked the sun never to set on Old Glory—as it was said constantly to illumine some British outpost. Most of all he wanted, as he kept writing his family, to "get into a scrap."

It is not on record, however, that John Mitchell actively opposed his son's desire to get at Aguinaldo. It is true that Harriet Mitchell wrote her son disparaging his new wish that the family pull wires. Yet when Billy's orders came, it is probable that their friend General Greely was behind them.

The laconic orders transferred Second Lieutenant William Mitchell to the Pacific Expeditionary Forces as a Signal Corps officer. Billy immediately bought all the books he could find on the Philippines. He had probably been impressed by the fact that on May Day the year before, when the Dewey news had flashed, the State and Navy Departments had found nothing in their files later than 1872 relating to the islands and that only the most specially instructed Americans had ever heard of them. Perhaps even the geography-minded Mitchells had been vague. Now, however, late in 1899 books and magazine articles on the subject were, figuratively speaking, a dime a dozen.

Stopping off at Milwaukee on his way to San Francisco, Billy is reported to have been treated as a hero by the younger elite of the city. A soldier back from that curious dream war was likely to be so met in any home town. There was little heroic competition. There was no hint of the weary boredom with which civilians welcomed the returned warriors of later episodes. For one thing the adventures such a boy as Mitchell had to relate were uncomplicated by technicalities. Anyone could understand the gallop of a cavalry charge, the sniper in an ambush, rifle fire that missed, the fording of a stream at night. There were no revetments or parapets or enfilades from machine-gun emplacements, no zero or H hours, no mine fields to be explored with detectors, no radar or flak or "mickey" or "snafu"; no "gook" jet on your tail at four o'clock in "MIG Alley."

The Milwaukee girls were said to be agog at the sight of Billy. Yet he was not a handsome lad in the conventional sense. He had a broad, high forehead; his face sloped in front to a small chin, though the jaws below his ears were prominent; his ears were flat against his head. His hair was abundant: its careful, accurate middle parting must have been difficult. His nose was long but straight; his mouth was full, suggesting the warm affections he was to know in later life. His eyes as we see them in photographs are obviously posed for severity: his friends said they were capable of hot flashes and gay laughter. His neck and shoulders were those of an athlete. He was not handsome but he was resplendent; his uniform was emblazed with the braid, buttons, epaulets, and gold ribbon which have since disappeared even from parade dress. And his poise, his walk, his bearing were such as a West Pointer might have envied.

The seven-week voyage westward from California was filled with study. He learned to name the trees, plants, birds, and insects of new jungles, the soundings of new harbors, the customs of semisavage tribes. He refreshed on signaling and telegraphy, read and lectured on military en-

The sinking of the *Ostfriesland*

General Mitchell directing the bombing of the ships, July, 1921

gineering. He wrote abundant reports on everything he learned and became extremely facile with his pen. Prolific writing became a lifelong habit and, while the millions of words he wrote—some of which contributed to his down-fall—made no approach to literary quality, his articles flooding a later press were direct, forthright, and readable to the interested. All this took the form in 1899 of letters home. Billy Mitchell always felt the need to express to someone every thought and experience: his family, then, was the normal recipient.

He landed in Luzon on November 10. He found himself in General Arthur MacArthur's division. In less than a week he was in the thick of the fighting. He wrote home in excitement about the "terrible shooting." In their attack on MacArthur's headquarters the insurgents won his immediate respect, though this was lost in later encounters. Mitchell was at once ordered to establish telegraphic communications and given virtually no equipment with which to do it. There was not even wire. He unwound wire from captured cannons, spliced it with barbed wire, made his own batteries with common salt for the saline solution, and received the faint messages by placing the wire end against his tongue and grounding his hand in the mud. He made insulators of dry bamboo and broken bottles. One of these he nailed accidentally, at night, to a roadside crucifix and, being a normally religious lad, was horrified in the morning at his mistake.

He showed early genius at improvisation. When he had inadequate pack animals, he used the native water buffalo. When uniforms gave out, he acquired enough from the enemy to equip his men and turned them inside out, so that they were not recognizable as Filipino outfits. He kept organizing side shows of his own, begged and secured orders for them, and went with small detachments on dangerous expeditions. It was, of course, that kind of war: perhaps the kind we have fought later gives a lieutenant less varied experience. According to his own account he captured with his own hands Aguinaldo's aide Mendoza, though Funston, who finally captured Aguinaldo himself, does not mention this.

With all these activities Mitchell found time to make friends with some naked Negritos and to go big-game hunting with them. In the Philippines, as elsewhere, he could never resist the opportunity to kill wild animals. His main target here was boar, but with scientific interest he seems also to have attacked alligators, snakes, and lizards. It was a wonderful war, precisely down Billy Mitchell's alley. Yet we wonder, as we follow him through life, if he did not in any war or any peace create his own alleys.

The show in the Philippines ended with Colonel Frederick Funston's ingenious and heroic capture of Emilio Aguinaldo. This has gone down in the history of the United States as one of the top exploits of old-time warfare. It is, of course, in as completely different a category from the ace flying of Eddie Rickenbacker or Doolittle's flight over Tokyo as if a thousand years lay between them.

When the war could no longer be fought successfully by a shattered Filipino army, its leader retired into an unknown mountain stronghold and from there directed harassing guerrilla operations against the Americans. This was intolerable to a disciplined army which followed the rules of so-called "civilized" warfare. Yet as long as Aguinaldo remained alive and free, the war must continue. Aguinaldo must be found, and it took an individualist, a lone wolf, an unorthodox soldier, to find him.

Billy Mitchell seems to have offered himself for the job, for it was his meat. He was turned down on account of his age. Shortly afterward he applied for leave. It was obvious to him that, unless he could follow the wild general to his lair, the Philippines held for him no further adventure. There was nothing cantankerous about Mitchell's act. It was inspired simply by his persistent, dominant restlessness, the perennial search for something new.

The leave was granted, and Mitchell left the Philippines for a long voyage through the Orient. Whether or not he foresaw that the future of the United States lay in and west of the Pacific and wanted, therefore, to learn what he could about it, he explored Japan, China, and India. He met his father in Cairo, and there was a general family reunion in Paris where the great exhibition of 1900 was beginning.

5

Top of the World

TODAY AMERICAN TROOPS are moved round the globe so rapidly that within a few weeks they are able to face an enemy almost anywhere. They are sent from sweltering heat to bitter frost, from dry, flat desert to steaming jungle or white-capped mountains with clothing and equipment for the new climate, and only the normal service gripes are heard. Climate-proof packaged rations prevent change from a home diet. Radio tells the outpost soldiers of a world series or the lighting of a Christmas tree while it is happening in New York or Washington, and Bing Crosby sings them to sleep in the snow or beneath low tropic stars.

In 1900 you moved from place to place in slow ships, in trains, on horseback, by dog sled, or on foot. The new place might be little known in its climate and topography, its harbors only sketchily charted, some of its rivers and mountain passes not yet mapped. We were ignorant enough about the Philippines when Admiral Dewey arrived in Manila Harbor. In 1901 Alaska was still an adventurer's dream. It would not have been surprising if the officers of the Signal Corps who had been stringing wires in the heavy heat of Luzon had felt a weakening of the knees when they

were ordered to spend a winter stringing wires in the frozen
valley of the Yukon.

Alaska, however, was more than a dream to General
Greely. He knew more about it than most Americans, and
it did not scare him. It was United States territory. The
government had bought it from Russia in 1867 and then
had forgotten it for thirty years. In 1897 the government
was reminded of it when news came that placer gold had
been found in an Alaskan region called the Klondike.
Thousands of Americans had rushed north to stake claims
just as they had rushed west to California in 1849. Because
so many of them had got lost, had moved out of all communication with the rest of the world, and had starved to
death, it seemed to the Arctic-conscious Chief Signal Officer that it was the government's responsibility to bring
some sort of civilization into this cold fringe of its empire.

By the turn of the century, when Hawaii and the Philippines had been occupied, Greely also saw Alaska's potential
strategic command of the Pacific. He could not foresee
the part the Aleutian Islands, which curve out like a thin
beard from Alaska's chin, would one day play in a war
with Japan. Nor could he guess that aircraft could one day
fly north from Alaska over the top of the world to western
Russia, ignoring the flat maps on which the ways of ships
were marked. He was, however, accustomed to turning
a globe under exploring fingers, and on it he saw Alaska's
relation to the Orient. It was not merely for the sake of the
gold seekers that he wanted to install a telegraph system
in Alaska. He wanted it for outposts of the Army. It was,
therefore, appropriate for the Army to build it.

Attempts had been made to do the job, and they had

failed. "Experts" had then said (as they so often do) that it was impossible. Greely disagreed. The word was not in his vocabulary. This conflict of opinion, however, did not inspire Congress to vote large sums of money to be buried in ice and snow. In 1900 Greely, fifty-six, went north in person to prove the experts wrong. It seems not to have occurred to him that the hardships of such a reconnaissance might be tough for a man of his age. Compared to the Arctic regions in which he had once been lost for many months, Alaska's climate was easy. He took the job in his stride and did it with characteristic thoroughness. It afforded him, he wrote in his modest report, "invaluable knowledge . . . as to topographical features of line construction, [and] it also confirmed his belief that such a line could be built and operated, despite the predictions of many persons of Alaskan experience that such work was impossible of execution."

Fortunately there is always more than one Greely in the world. There were men in the Signal Corps who had the same sort of adventurous courage and enough confidence in their chief and in themselves to volunteer for this hazardous task. Some of them were still in the Philippines, where the climate was supposed in those days to "thin the blood" and decrease resistance to cold. One of them was, in 1901, in hot Fort Myer, Virginia, which for him was hotter and more uncomfortable because of the job he was required to do there.

In the summer of 1901 Billy Mitchell "belonged," as they say, to Uncle Sam. Coming back with his family from Europe, thus circling the earth, he had been offered the career post of first lieutenant in the Regular Army of the

United States. This step up from the Volunteers had been possible only after he had passed his twenty-first birthday. He had toyed with other careers for a time but only as a man will juggle tennis balls in his hand before his first swift serve at the beginning of a set. His heart had been in the Army for three years, and it was inevitable that the rest of his body and soul should follow it.

Belonging to Uncle Sam, however, did (and still does) limit a man's freedom of action. If you are ordered to count wool socks or file papers, you do not explain that you are better fitted for something else. At Fort Myer, Virginia, the daily monotony of close-order drill must have seemed to Mitchell as stultifying as counting socks. It is, of course, a part of every officer's experience; most of them accept it tranquilly enough. It is an easy, lazy business well adapted to a mind that hates to think. Soldiers' legs are like the levers of machines; commands are like the flick of a gear-shift. But Mitchell's temperament was already that of the lone eagle which he became, and the work was gradually driving him, as we would say, "nuts."

He heard of Greely's plan and asked that he be sent north. His request evidently answered a question that had been worrying the general. The reports of the Chief Signal Officer reveal Greely's concern in finding enough technically equipped officers for this kind of work. To expect officers of the line of the Army to install a telegraph system was like expecting a boxer to build a house. The Signal Corps must do it. But at that time there were only thirty-five officers in the entire Signal Corps (including Greely), and there were doubts in the general's mind about how many of them would weather an Alaskan winter. To have a volunteer rush forward out of the blue—a young, vigorous, and resourceful lieutenant who had proved his way with men in adverse conditions—must have been, to say the least, a relief.

Mitchell's orders came through quickly. He was to proceed at once to Alaska. He was to take with him a detachment of men from Fort Myer and "distribute" them among the army stations on the Yukon. This would be his "military duty." But his real mission was to report on why the people who had already started on the telegraph work were so slow.

He embarked at Seattle in July. Seattle in 1901 was a gay frontier town, the first stop on the way home for men who had mined a fortune in the Klondike. One had just arrived when Mitchell got there. Still in his miner's clothes, he had gone to the best hotel and ordered dinner. The waiter preferred to attend to the well-dressed guests first until the miner laid a pocketful of gold on the table and shouted, "I'm hungry. Bring me two thousand dollars' worth of ham and eggs!"

The next morning this astonishing character hired all the carriages in town and invited everyone who wanted to go on a tour of saloons for free drinks. "Soon," Mitchell wrote, "the crowd was tremendous, not only overflowing the insides of the hacks but occupying all the room on top. A few busses were pressed into service but these proved inadequate. As a last resort, about fifteen hearses were obtained and filled to capacity."

Mitchell's soldiers, whose pay was fifteen dollars a month, watched this extravaganza. The temptation to desert and join the Klondike miners must have been compelling. But

Mitchell had learned the army trick of picking his sergeant with care, and with the discipline this war-trained noncom exercised not a man was lost.

The Alaska that Mitchell found when he got to the area where the telegraph was planned was not the Alaska he had heard of. It was hot in August and there were mosquitoes. Traveling down the Yukon, Mitchell, with his quick observation and his persistent inquisitiveness, learned more in a few weeks than the average traveler would have gathered in as many months. He made friends with Malemiut Indians and learned their habits, how they protected themselves from the winters, and about their clothes, boats, hunting, and fishing. To his question, asked of Indians, American prospectors, trappers, traders, or soldiers in the lonely army garrisons, "What do you do in the winter?" the invariable answer was "We hole in." Like hibernating animals! The soldiers, especially, had never dreamed of working in winter: they shivered at the thought.

Mitchell watched them working in the summer. As there were virtually no roads, everything had to be transported by pack animals. These mules or horses traversing swamps and mossy morasses sank to their knees under a heavy burden. They could, therefore, carry only 200 pounds on their backs. But in winter Mitchell figured, with the ground frozen and covered with snow, they could pull 2,000 pounds on sledges.

He returned in October. According to his own succinct account:

I submitted a report of my observations in Alaska to General Greely . . . to the effect that the people trying to build telegraph lines stayed in the house too much in the winter, and that if they got out and worked when it was cold, the lines could be built. Whereupon Gen. Greely ordered me to return to Alaska and build them and I was delighted with the prospect.

Mitchell hardly had time to organize and provide himself with proper equipment before he was back in a very different Alaska. In the White Pass, the approach to Dawson, the snow was 40 to 50 feet deep and the thermometer registered 35 degrees below zero. He came over the pass by sledge with relays of horses every 25 miles. His final destination was Fort Egbert, a little army garrison near the Canadian border. It was from here he would drive his line south to the coast at Prince William Sound, where connection would be made with what he had already learned to call "the outside."

He found the garrison "in rather a poor state of discipline." There were a great many recruits and few older noncommissioned officers. All were "holed in" for the winter. They did nothing whatever except occasionally visit nearby Eagle City, where they usually got into trouble. Many of them, as the long nights came on, succumbed to melancholy: here and there in the Alaskan army posts there were suicides in this season. "It is difficult," Mitchell wrote, "to handle a group of men without giving them plenty of work."

American soldiers who were stationed at weather bases in Greenland in World War II can form some faint picture of winter life in such a garrison. Yet in Greenland there were the arrivals of four-motored transport planes to land supplies, bring stateside newspapers two days old, and break the monotony; there was the constant radio; there were movies and an occasional show staged by an air-borne USO; there were thrilling rescues after plane crashes on the icecap. In Fort Egbert in January there was nothing to cheer the little group of weary men in the twenty-hour nights beyond the rare comings of dog sleds with stale provisions or of the mail carrier with letters months old.

These soldiers must have welcomed Billy Mitchell with special pleasure. Tired as they must have been of the sight of one another's drawn faces, this young officer, glowing with delight at his new adventure, surely brightened their darkness. His quick imagination gilding an inexhaustible fund of stories, his ingenuity at inventing games and pastimes of all sorts, his excitement over dog teams and hunting, his interest in every technic, his startling youth and tireless vigor, and, above all, his mission to bring them into immediate touch with the homeland would have been extremely tonic to such despairing "holed-in" souls.

The plan was for him to move south, surveying the telegraph route and transporting poles and supplies to be cached along the way. With him would go a detachment of soldiers; dog sleds and pack animals would carry the equipment. When summer came and the ground thawed, holes for the poles could be dug and the wire strung. All the necessary tons of supplies would be in place; there would be no laborious transport through the mud, heat, and insects. At the other end of the projected line—at Valdez—another officer was to move north; he and Mitchell would meet somewhere between. They started simultaneously on their first survey in the first week of January, 1902. The mercury was frozen in that week: only the al-

cohol thermometers showed 60 degrees below zero at Fort
Egbert. Mitchell moved with two dog teams and two sleds.
He found his route with a prismatic compass and blazed
a trail which he would move over later with the heavy
supplies.

A volume would scarcely be sufficient to record his adventures through the next year and a half. Happily, Mitchell kept full notes. Late in his life he did make a book of
these, but other events had become so important that it
was never published. The manuscript, however, gives us
the sense of high danger through which he moved and the
gay courage with which he met it.

He learned early of the tricks that kept men and dogs
from freezing. There were the perils of tight clothing, of
overexertion which induced sweating, of falling into water,
of drinking liquor, of dogs getting trapped in their harness;
there was the need of sure means of making a fire—axes,
matches, kerosene, candles. And Mitchell learned, too,
that a wise dog can save a man's life.

Two stories stand out from the rest because they reveal
the sort of contradiction that we find throughout Mitchell's
life. In one we see the better known tough bravery and
quick thinking a short step from certain death; in the other
there is a patience, a tolerance, and a kind of tenderness
which only his intimates knew.

There was a spot on the edge of the Tokyo River where
ice had formed in layers with water between. The top layer
was too thin when Mitchell and his assistant Emmet passed
over it with their sleds; dogs and men fell through.

In one place [he wrote] I broke through with my sled, clear
to my shoulders, and if my leader Pointer had not gotten a foot-

hold and pulled out Hunter, the second dog, and the rest of the team I would probably have been there yet.

But getting out of the water was more immediately dangerous than staying in. After freeing the dogs from their harness, therefore, he jumped back into the water and called to Emmet to chop down a tree on the bank so that they could start a fire. Emmet's ax handle, brittle with the cold, broke. Mitchell jumped ashore, told Emmet to get into the water, lit two candles, and started work on the tree with a second ax. This also broke. Emmet then took his turn with a third, last ax and got the tree down, "stripping off the branches in a second and getting them in a blaze." With the fire they thawed their clothes, already "stiff as boards," and finally dried them, after which they rounded up the dogs, mended the broken harness, cooked and ate a large meal—all, apparently, in the greatest gaiety.

The other story is of the saving, not of a life, but of a mind. Once, before starting on one of his many trips, Mitchell got a message from the Commander of the Canadian Mounted Police in Dawson that a certain Signal Corps major was on his way up to inspect the work. The message said that the major "was acting strangely."

When Major F arrived, it was obvious to Mitchell that this was understatement. Through the night this officer, who had been a close friend of Mitchell in the States, talked of hearing voices and of being pursued by a "gang of rough men" who were out to kill him and would certainly do so at the first opportunity. Mitchell listened sympathetically and promised protection, but the prospect of working with such a man for a long period in wilderness was hardly inviting.

I was confronted [Mitchell wrote] with a difficult problem. Unquestionably Major F had lost his mind. If we confined him or restrained him physically, he would certainly go all to pieces and be incurably insane for the rest of his life. But if I got him out in the wilderness where he would get plenty of fresh air and exercise, hunting and fishing, and be in an entirely different scene, I thought I might get him over it. So I suggested that we start on the trip for the Tanana River the next morning.

All went well while they were alone together. But whenever they met a group of workers or Indians, the major's fears of "rough men" came back and he would sit in the camps or prowl about with loaded pistols.

"Of course it was a dangerous thing to be with a man in his condition and armed to the teeth, but I hoped to effect a cure."

Mitchell's tact, which must have been almost that of a trained psychiatrist, brought them through. The major was sent to a hospital at the end of the journey, and after a year of treatment he made a full recovery.

By early summer, 1903, the telegraph lines were completed. The parties from the north and south had met and joined their wires. Mitchell's section was 125 miles. General Greely's report states that he "carried his surveys and lines along the Good-pasture River across a country that had never before been trodden by the foot of a white man." In his 1902 report the general was unable to maintain the cool, dry tenor.

The toil and hardships experienced . . . cannot be fully appreciated by anyone unfamiliar with Alaskan trails. Suffice it to say that every pound of food, forage, tentage, etc., wire, insulators, or line material has to be moved by pack animals over a trail so rough that an animal can hardly travel 15 miles a day.

Cold and rapid glacial streams, swampy morasses, tangled underbrush, steep declivities, narrow canyons, thick timber, and sharp ridges alternate to tax the strength of man and animal to the utmost. The monotony of the life is exceedingly trying after the novelty of scenery disappears. Rarely is any large game or even bird life seen, and humanity, whether in the shape of prospector or Indian, appears infrequently. When to these conditions are added the physical discomforts attendant on frequent falls of rain in summer and snow in winter, with high, cutting winds, it requires firmness of purpose to persevere to the end.

In the report for 1903 he pays tribute to the soldiers whom the work saved from suicidal melancholy:

It is doubted whether in the peaceful annals of the Army there have been met with nobler fortitude by the enlisted men equal conditions of hardship and privation.

Mitchell, promoted to captain, left Alaska in July, 1903. He was not yet twenty-four. In Denver, to which he was transferred, he pursued some of the studies he had taken up during the long periods of darkness in Alaska when work on the trails was impossible.

These studies were of Signal Corps technics. Prominent among these were balloons. The armies had used balloons since the Civil War for observation. The subject fascinated Mitchell, but it would have fascinated any young man who had dedicated himself to this branch of the service. In most of the stories about Billy Mitchell, these investigations of his are emphasized as the beginning of his interest in aviation. This is unlikely. He found radiotelegraphy, then in its infancy, equally compelling and devoted much of his time in the next ten years to its study.

He was probably aware of the event, which occurred

some six months after he left Alaska, when two brother bicycle mechanics of Dayton, Ohio, launched a contraption on the wind-swept sands of Kitty Hawk which changed the face of the world. Perhaps General Greely, who had followed with intense interest the behavior of machines which were heavier than the air since the days of Otto Lilienthal, called it to his attention. Yet in the twelve years from that December day in 1903 William Mitchell never tried to fly.

6

Grounded America

As we explore the record of this soldier's life, we are surprised at the slow, gradual approach he made to aviation. That is because he has been blown up by enthusiastic hero worshipers into a great flyer, a kind of super ace. Actually his flying was incidental. He learned to fly, finally, because he was the kind of officer who would never order anyone to do something he could not do himself and because he always insisted on knowing the technical detail of every instrument he commanded others to use. But his personal performances in the air were nothing compared with his deep understanding of strategy and the tactics of all arms. It will be well for us to think of him, not as we think of men like Eddie Rickenbacker, Frank Luke, Joe Wehner, Pierpont Hamilton, Harl Pease, and all the bright galaxy of air-battle heroes, but as a general, a planner of operations, a revolutionist of the military art, a crusader for air power, a philosopher, and a prophet of aviation.

He became these things because his basic training was on the ground. It is true he had much of the temperament of a flyer. He was quick-thinking, quick-coordinating, and daring, and preferred lone-eagle exploits to close-order discipline. And he was a passionate devotee of sport. Flying *was* a sport in its early days in America and very little else: he might easily have been tempted into the air as many other young Army officers were. Fortunately, he was constantly busy and deeply interested in other things: in radio, balloon observation, photography, and all the business of the Signal Corps; in wide travel and remote missions and, finally, in grand strategy and a kind of "global" thinking in military terms which was unusual in his day. Fortunately, too, his orders in those years were for special jobs for which he was temperamentally adapted, and they led him into a varied and exciting life.

In the year after Alaska he was at Fort Leavenworth experimenting with kites for the catching of wireless messages. On one of them he got a signal from a ship 1,900 miles away and set a world's record for distance. He used the kites also for aerial photography. The following year he became an instructor on communications at the Leavenworth staff college, and his lectures were made into army textbooks. In 1906 he was sent to San Francisco to restore communications after the great earthquake and fire, and in 1908 he graduated with distinction from the Army School of the Line and from the Army Staff College. These last two achievements were proof that his study had covered the whole science of war, and their importance to his later career was greater than the sum of all his flying hours.

During these years he had found time for his favorite sports, hunting and polo. He had schooled horses and trained them in jumping. How he fitted these things into such an incessantly active army life was a wonder to all who knew him. He would take days off in the midst of his missions, chase jaguar and deer through the mountains just as earnestly as he had strung wires or flown his antennae- or camera-bearing kites, and return to his work without missing a beat of the strenuous rhythm of his life. Also, in an interval of work, he had married a girl whose mother had long been a friend of Mrs. Mitchell, but even on his honeymoon he was back at work exploring military defenses in the Caribbean.

In 1909 he was sent back to the Philippines, and the fascination of the Far East, with all the problems that he knew were even then shaping themselves for America's future, gripped him again. He asked for leave from his job as signal officer and spent some two years studying the dim blueprint of the troubles he would not live to see. He worked out in his mind the multitude of "ifs" that made up the menacing mystery of the Pacific. With them he envisioned the possible wars that would emerge in time from the hatreds of Oriental peoples for each other and especially for the Western foreigner.

He went to Japan, China, Korea, and Manchuria; took the pulse of their peoples; measured their civilization and their barbarism and their strengths and weaknesses in terms of strategy and defense, of politics and economy, of spiritual force and bodily hunger. Among the Mitchell papers in the Library of Congress are photographs he took in Mukden, which are too horrible to print, of men stripped naked and beheaded and left to rot on the fields as warnings to other offenders against police power. These are evidence of the dark secrets this young captain's inquiring mind penetrated in lonely and barbaric places. All his investigations of these years, written up in his usual voluminous reports, supplied the War Department with valuable records. If their value had been properly estimated, they might have led to preparations for the attack which thirty years later brought such disaster to American arms.

At that time, however, the War Department seemed to be interested in everything except war. It was enormously interested in the Panama Canal, which the Army had been digging for eight years and which was nearly finished. It was interested in Mexico, where a revolution was in progress and American business interests were endangered, and in the troubles of Nicaragua and Haiti. It was interested in radio. But to the subject which in 1912 was causing a fever of interest in all the war ministries of Europe, it turned an almost deaf ear. That subject was military aviation.

The reason aviation developed so fast in Europe between 1908 and 1913 was because the threat of war was always present. France and Germany were constantly eying each other across a disputed frontier. Russia, still smarting from her defeat by Japan in 1905, was working to build up strength to prevent such a thing from happening again. Bulgaria, Italy, Turkey, and Greece were actually fighting by 1913. England was more detached because of the little strip of water she had always relied on for protection; yet even in England the threat of war was not wholly discounted.

Therefore, in 1908, when Wilbur Wright put on a demonstration of the airplane in Le Mans, France, the news spread like fire over the continent—not that here was an exciting new sport but that here was a highly important weapon. Within a year the governments of France, Germany, and Russia were appropriating substantial sums of money for aviation; they were designing and building air-craft and organizing air forces.

On the other hand, when Orville Wright almost simul-taneously put on a similar demonstration at Fort Myer, Virginia, before an official group of American Army officers, our preoccupied War Department showed faint interest and the "peanut" appropriation of thirty thousand dollars was not increased. The general public regarded the affair as a sporting event, and sports promoters spent the follow-ing years in putting on air shows in which daredevil fliers put on stunts and were killed by the dozen. The United States, in short, was simply not war-minded. Protected for generations by the oceans and by the British navy, Ameri-cans did not even consider ever having to fight a foreign war.

It is true that Orville had bad luck. A plane he had built for the Army crashed after several successful perform-ances; the Army aviation pioneer, Thomas Selfridge, was killed and Orville himself was seriously injured. A few farsighted young men in the Signal Corps insisted that another be ordered. It was delivered a year later. In July, 1910, therefore, the War Department was able to list the air strength of the United States as: 1 officer, 9 enlisted men, 1 Wright "aeroplane," 1 Baldwin airship, and 3 cap-tive balloons. This so impressed the Department and Con-gress that the following March the fabulous sum of $125,-000 was appropriated for "air operations" for the fiscal year of 1912!

By 1912 Captain Mitchell had come back from his far wanderings. Had he then remained in the Signal Corps, he would certainly have turned all his energy and thought to this thrilling new Signal Corps activity. But destiny had other plans for him. He was awarded the unheard-of honor for an officer only thirty-two years old of appointment to the General Staff of the Army. It was reward for all the work of his life, his exhaustive study, his wide explorations, and his sure talent. It was an exacting job, analyzing intelligence from all over the world, reading reports from military attachés with foreign governments, and planning maneuvers.

This was the start of his first real interest in an American air force. That he was still far from being the crusader or prophet he later became is evident from what happened that August. He was asked to give before the Military Affairs Committee of the House of Representatives his opinion as to whether aviation should be taken out of the hands of the Signal Corps and a new aviation corps set up as part of the line of the Army. His opinion was asked because the Signal Corps was his permanent branch of the service, from which he was temporarily detached to serve on the General Staff. He was put on the spot then, facing a conflict of loyalties.

The Signal Corps was his first love. The Signal Corps had started military aviation in the United States, and Mitchell was jealous of this honor. He did not think it was right, he said, to "disgruntle" the Signal Corps officers who had worked so hard to build our air force, tiny as it was. This is the only public demonstration he ever seems to have made of this kind of service jealousy.

But he also gave some more cogent reasons for his opinion. No other branch, he said, had the necessary technical knowledge and equipment or the responsibility for ob-

servation—then the primary task of aviation. No other
branch had aviators or facilities for training aviators. He
was backed up in this opinion by Lieutenants Henry H.
Arnold, Thomas Milling, and Benjamin Foulois, three of
the foremost fliers and aviation enthusiasts of the day.

Many years later, when he was accused of the horrible
army offense of changing his mind, he said, "I never made
a greater mistake in my life." He did not apologize or explain. He was not the kind to nurse regrets or remorse. He
simply laughed at his error as if to say, "You see how little
I knew in those days; how much I've learned since!"

Yet in that same testimony in August, 1913, he said one
thing which clearly shows the trend of his mind.

The actual flying is a small part of it; it is only from 30 to 50
per cent of the whole thing. . . . Unless the flyer has studied
the military features of it, he would not be able to understand
and state what he sees . . . he must be able to tell, when he
sees the enemy's movements, what they will do afterward. He
must have knowledge of the military art and of service with
large bodies of troops.

Let us now take a brief look at what had been going on
abroad from 1908 to 1913. While the United States government had in these years spent a total of $435,000 and
had finally built up a force of 28 planes, good and bad,
flying and grounded, Germany had spent $28,000,000 and
had a force of 400 planes in the air and many more on
order. France had spent $22,000,000 and also had 400
planes; Russia $12,000,000 and had 300 planes; Italy
$8,000,000 and had 200 planes; and so on down to Japan,
Bulgaria, and Greece with 80 planes each and government
expenditures running from $500,000 to $1,500,000.

The American War Department had these figures before it. It knew that the United States stood fourteenth in the list of money spent and twelfth in the number of planes. It knew that for the year 1913 alone France and Germany each had appropriated $5,000,000 for aviation. Yet in the War Department's annual report for 1913, the Secretary of War made this astonishing statement, "It has seemed wise to me this year, in view of other more urgent necessities, not to ask for any large appropriation for these services."

He asked, in fact, for the same old $125,000!

These are the dry statistics. They reflect the old American complacency. But behind the statistics, working on the shoestring their government had given them, there were men with spirit—daredevils and heroes—angry men who were humiliated to see America fall so far behind in a force they had come to realize would one day be necessary to survival. Reading now of their exploits or remembering them, we know that our air power was built by men, not by machines or government; by daring individual fliers who learned their techniques as they flew, not by engineers with slide rules or the tooling of a production line; by boyish lieutenants who fought for their aircraft and even sometimes for their flying time.

They were almost all lieutenants, the heroes of those early days: Humphreys and Lahm soloing after three hours' teaching by Wilbur Wright in October, 1909, Crissy who demonstrated live bombing, Foulois with his 106-mile non-stop flight, Milling with his world endurance record in 1911, Henry H. Arnold reaching the dizzy altitude record of 6,540 feet in 1912, and Milling again in that year piloting the plane in which Captain Chandler demonstrated that aerial machine-gun firing was possible. We shall meet these people later: it was inevitable for most of them to cross at some point the path of William Mitchell.

When war came in Europe in the late summer of 1914, Mitchell became wholly absorbed in it. It was then that he saw what the French and the Germans could do with the expensive aviation equipment they had built up so assiduously for six years. It was then that he saw an entirely new kind of war which would scrap all the previous military thinking through history: which would nullify fortifications, reduce sea power, set a whole new pattern for intelligence, and, finally, bring civil populations under fire.

In 1916 he learned to fly at the Curtiss Flying School on the Potomac. In his first solo flight he found that the air was the element in which, from then on, his mind must move whether his body moved in it or not.

Some six months after he had become a licensed pilot, he obtained leave to go abroad. The itch to see a war first-hand—and the largest war the world had ever known—was too much for him. He arrived in Spain in March, 1917. On the sixth of April the news came to him that his country was going to fight.

7

The Eyes of the Armies

"I WANT TO KNOW ABOUT your organization, General, your equipment and your system of supply. It is important, too, for me to know about your operations against the enemy as we shall want to participate in them."

The tall, erect chief of British aviation looked down at the young American major with an expression between annoyance and amusement.

"That's a large order," he said. "How much time can you give to it?"

"Well," the American said, "we could do up the first part of it this afternoon and evening. Then tomorrow morning, we can start in——"

The general interrupted. His habit was brief, brusque speech, and he was not accustomed to wasting time with majors whatever their nationality.

"Look here, Major Mitchell," he said, "is it your idea that I have no other duty but to show you round and answer your questions?"

Billy Mitchell did not salute and about-face. He continued smiling and said, "No, General Trenchard. But it *is* my idea that you have such an excellent organization that it should not need your leadership for the space of a day or two, no matter how serious the conditions may be."

The general looked at him a moment with his fiercest expression and suddenly burst out laughing.

"I expect, young man," he said, "that you are going to get what you want."

They started then on a tour of British air headquarters in France.

Major General Hugh Trenchard was, at the time of this meeting, the great British pioneer in military flying. Because he had been a regular army officer for twenty years when World War I began and had fought in South Africa, he had the essential ground training. He had learned to fly in 1912 and had been an instructor in flying until the war broke out. In a year he had risen from major to major general: when Mitchell met him, he was head of the Royal Flying Corps. At that time, May, 1917, the work of aircraft had been largely observation with occasional haphazard dropping of bombs. There had been a few unplanned dogfights with pilots shooting rifles at each other. Trenchard was for organized attack on enemy planes by formations of aircraft designed for the purpose. He was the father of the fighter squadron. But he was also, even in that early time, a champion of strategic bombing: the destruction of enemy installations far in the rear. His name was a household word in France, and when the French expressed this kind of feeling for an Englishman, it meant something more than respect for military efficiency. It meant affection for some quality of heart and spirit.

"The Germans," said Trenchard as they walked, "still think of the airplane as a defensive weapon. That is why the work they have actually accomplished on the British front is about 4 per cent of what we have done. The one exception to this is their night bombing. They have inflicted thousands of casualties on our troops in bivouac by a new twin-engine aircraft called a Gotha. We must learn this."

The general told him the British had 2,000 planes on the line. To an American who knew that no American plane could reach France for many months, this was at once impressive and disheartening. But Mitchell, every step of the way, was building in his mind, not a pile of facts about what aircraft could do, but a great architectural plan of organization. He saw, as Trenchard talked, not merely planes but formations of planes; not merely formations—orderly, disciplined, and purposeful—but vast armies on the ground, systems of trenches, railheads and marshalling yards behind the trenches, supply ports behind the rail terminals, and ships on the sea beyond the ports. He saw war covering the world and reaching into every far place of it with the little, fabric-covered, wooden-strutted planes at the point of the wedge. But he must have seen, too, enlarged shadows of these planes, forecasts of the giants of the sky that were to come.

Most of all, perhaps, Billy Mitchell saw the future pattern of his own career, for that was Trenchard's pattern. We all, at some point in our lives, are inspired by someone, by some spoken or printed word, toward a life path. It is likely that the most formative influences in his case were those of Greely and Trenchard and the Italian air prophet Giulio Douhet. It is certain that he was at a crossroads that May afternoon in the buzzing center of British air strategy and that he saw, before his visit was over, the great vista ahead of the hills and valleys over which he would pass. It was still foggy, to be sure, but it was adventurous, exciting.

Mitchell's authority in bearding the winged lion, Trenchard, in his den was partly official and partly justified by some lone-eagle exploits during the scant month he had been in France. He was still a staff officer and had a good Signal Corps record. In Paris he had joined a small group of preliminary American "observers" of the war. But he had then gone out on his own to the French front and persuaded French officers to let him sit in a trench under fire and, more important, to allow him to be the first American officer to fly over the lines. It was a time, to be sure, when any uniformed American was kissed on both cheeks and otherwise embarrassed by every French officer from Pétain down. Mitchell had been dined and wined and asked so many questions that it had been hard even for him, the adroit questioner, to get a word in edgewise.

"When will the American soldiers come?"

"How soon will American aircraft be at the front?"

"How many thousand *avions?*"

"When will the General Pershing come?"

"We already have *Père* Joffre! Now we shall have *Père* Shing, too!"

"How fast are American factories turning out airplanes and engines?"

"Will the Americans send us spruce wood for our own *avions?*"

Mitchell had trouble answering. The word from home was confused. All that came over in newspapers and dispatches was that the American war effort would be "pro-digious." He may have translated this into *formidable* for the Frenchmen, but it is probable that he was cautious. From General Pershing's war diary we learn the actual state of American air preparedness in May, 1917:

> The situation . . . as to aviation was such that every American ought to feel mortified to hear it mentioned. Out of 65 officers and about 1000 men in the Air Service Section of the Signal Corps, there were 35 officers who could fly. With the exception of five or six officers, none of them could have met the requirement of modern battle conditions. . . .
> We could boast 55 training planes . . . all . . . valueless for service at the front. Of these 55 planes . . . the National Advisory Committee for Aeronautics . . . advised that 51 were obsolete and the other 4 obsolescent. We could not have put a single squadron in the field, although it was estimated later that we should eventually need at least 300 sqaudrons, each to be composed on the average of some 24 officers, 180 men and 18 airplanes, besides a large reserve of planes for replacements.

From British headquarters Mitchell returned to the hotel in Paris where the American mission lived. He found a promotion to lieutenant colonel awaiting him. Wearing his new insignia, he left again and flew along the front of the Fourth French Army in the Champagne. He was presented with the *Croix de guerre*. He visited the French aviation schools at Avord. He kept meeting American volunteers who had enlisted in a French unit.

> There are a good many Americans . . . [he wrote in his diary] in the French Foreign Legion, probably a couple of hundred of them. These are the men that I am so anxious to get for our own Aviation as they will have several months' start on any we can get from the United States.

On the thirteenth of June, General Pershing arrived to set up his command of the American Expeditionary Force. It was a gala day. All Paris turned out with the tears and the flowers it reserves for these emotional occasions. In Mitchell's diary a note shows him preoccupied with the clothes he should wear.

Churchill [Major Marlborough Churchill, USA] and I had been wearing Sam Browne belts [unauthorized]. We had also bought blouses . . . that covered the seat of our trousers instead of the variety used by our Army, which stopped a little below the waist belt. These blouses or "Mother Hubbards" . . . were popularly known as "Seymours" because you could "see more" of the seat of a person's trousers. . . . Churchill and I discussed whether we should wear the uniforms we had made in Europe. . . . I determined to do so anyway and appeared with a Sam Browne belt on.

Anyone who remembers the stiff costume that regulations demanded—looking more like the "monkey suits" of chauffeurs than officers' uniforms—will understand Mitchell's impatience. In this loose, flaring, big-pocketed tunic he went at once to Pershing's Aviation Officer, Major Townsend Dodd, whom he was delighted to see he ranked, and demanded to see the general. He was invited to dinner with the formidable "Black Jack" and apparently gained the confidence of this hard-boiled but harassed commander at once. This is implied in Mitchell's diary, to which he usually confided matters of personal pride, and it is borne out by the general's later behavior. Probably the first indication was the fact that Pershing did not instantly send him home to change his clothes. Never in our military history was there a greater stickler for regulation dress, and many a high-ranking officer had smarted under his rebukes.

During the summer Mitchell acquired a powerful car and became, it is said, a terror on Napoleon's roads. His cruising speed of 80 to 90 kilometers an hour was an achievement even for a Mercedes of the day with its muffler cut out. His August diary mentions an incident which began a long friendship. He was driving a French officer. Behind them was Major Dodd, driven by a chauffeur. Mitchell's car broke down, and his own mechanic could do nothing about it. Dodd's smart young driver came up and took over. Soon the engine was going and Mitchell, who had an intuition for potential fliers, asked who he was.

"He is an American automobile racer. A champion. The general wanted him."

"Name?" asked Mitchell.

"Eddie, sir," said the chauffeur.

"Any other name?"

"Rickenbacker."

And Mitchell remembered. If there was anyone qualified by mechanical knowledge, daring, and love of speed to become an ace in the air, here was the man.

In that same August, Mitchell's impatience was stirred by the bloody, static nature of the war, so grim, so indecisive, in that summer when hope was fading all over the Allied world. His diary recorded one of his moments of reflection:

[The War] is a slaughterhouse performance from beginning to end on the ground. . . . Maybe one side makes a few yards

Library of Congress

With a Signal Corps group (Mitchell kneeling at right)

Library of Congress

Mitchell's record-breaking dog team in Alaska

"He learned early of the tricks that kept man . . . from freezing."

On a boar hunt in France

or maybe a mile and thousands of men are killed. It is not war, it is simply slaughter.

War is decided by getting at the vitals of the enemy, that is, to shoot him in the heart. This kind of war is like clipping off one finger, then a toe, then an ear, then his nose and gradually eating into his vitals.

The eating was certainly being done by Germany. All the background signs were bad. The Russian army had collapsed, and plans were being laid for a new Russia which would repudiate all alliance with the West. The sounds of mutiny in French camps could not be muffled. Submarines were taking their tolls on the oceans. The only hope was borne by "the slender column of our khaki-clad regulars," as Brand Whitlock described the Fourth-of-July parade in Paris when "French soldiers in their light blue trotted beside them, as closely as they could get, looking at them with almost childish interest and wonder, as boys trot hurrying beside a circus parade." That was all, the slender column, the unsoiled uniforms, the bright new American flag.

Billy Mitchell may have been moved by this parade, but he was not deeply impressed. He was assuredly neither moved nor impressed by the thunderous promises, which blew across the Atlantic, of the enormous aircraft production said to be afoot at home. Six hundred and forty million dollars had been appropriated. Gigantic fleets of American airplanes would be in the skies over France in no time at all. We would win the war immediately with all this superior air power. Mitchell knew that these claims were "utterly ridiculous" and that it would be "manifestly impossible for the United States to really put any efficient air units into the field before the summer of 1918, and even then they will have to be equipped with either French or British airplanes."

As fall came on, Mitchell went back whenever he could to his old passion.

In my spare moments I took every opportunity to hunt with the inhabitants of the [Upper Marne] valley. . . . There was a bounty of fifty francs on each wild boar. Whenever I killed one I took the bounty and used it to entertain the old men at luncheon.

The "old men" were hunters who could no longer hunt but loved to tell tales of their young exploits. Mitchell made close friends of them as well as of the boys with whom he stalked the woods.

One night he was driving along a dark road toward Chaumont at 60 miles an hour. Suddenly, directly ahead, he saw a herd of fierce, wild boar crossing the road. Instead of jamming on his brakes, he stepped hard on the gas driving at top speed into the slithering mass. When he had run through them, he stopped the car and backed to the point of contact.

Looking to one side of the road, I found one wild boar stone dead and on the other side of the road one stunned and lying there gnashing his teeth. I got a hammer out of the tool box as quickly as possible and killed him with one blow on the head. . . . We now had two fine young wild boar which I tied, one on each side of the car. . . .

He was billeted at this time in an old French château at Chamarande, near the Chaumont headquarters.

We gave a dinner in the state dining room . . . with these wild boars served in the old French style. It was a splendid feast, the night was cold outside and the guests came wrapped from head to foot in their furs. We had great wood fires in the large salon and good warm drinks to dispel the cold. Generals Liggett, Treat and Kennedy came with us and we had a delightful evening.

It is likely that such affairs assisted this lieutenant colonel's success with what we call the "top brass."

Nevertheless, troubles were brewing for Billy Mitchell at this very moment. There was no difficulty with Pershing or any of the commanders of skeleton army corps that was forming in the field. Nor was there any particular conflict with General W. L. Kenly, Chief of Air Service, who was in command of equipment and supply as well as combat and who had appointed Mitchell Commander of the Air Service in the Zone of the Advance, where he wanted to be. Mitchell was handling the few young American aviators who were already flying Breguet and Nieuport planes well enough and planning operations.

But back in Washington the armchair strategists were making and running their own war. It is a singular thing that this so often happens during the operations of the American armed forces. The "grand old men" in Washington looked at their maps and pictures, figured that what the men in the field were doing was all wrong, and remade the war nearer to their hearts' desire. And General Pershing and his staff, who could see the Germans in the air, could take it and like it.

Just as our organization began to work smoothly [Mitchell wrote in November], . . . a shipload of Aviation officers ar-

rived under Brigadier General Foulois. There were over one
hundred of them, almost none of them had ever seen an airplane. . . . Foulois, I am told, has orders from the President
to General Pershing to put him in charge of Aviation in Europe. . . .

Neither Pershing nor Mitchell had anything against
Foulois. He, at least, had been a pioneer flier. But the
hundred officers who, Pershing said, kept "running around
in circles" upset the applecart for the veterans. They
strutted about, giving fantastic orders out of a sense of
their own importance. They occupied army quarters and
consumed army rations and did nothing but confuse the
organization that in Mitchell's opinion operated so
smoothly.

Mitchell had by this time become a convinced champion
of an independent department of the government for air.
He reports in his diary a proposed cable which the experts
in the field urged the commanding general to send to
Washington as follows:

To harmonize interests and concentrate all efforts I strongly
favor establishment of air service department whose head shall
be member of executive cabinet charged with all matters per-
taining to American Air Service. His Assistants to be Chief of
the Army Air Service, Chief of the Navy Air Service and a member of the Munitions Board or corresponding organization.

Pershing

The cable, Mitchell comments without explanation, was
never sent.

"If a plan of this kind," he wrote, "had been adopted
and followed it would have saved millions of dollars, hun-

dreds of pilots' lives and undoubtedly shortened the war."

This excerpt from the diary—not altogether easy to understand at this point—concerns us more vitally than anything else in this record if we are to come clear on Mitchell's life. It is the key to all his later effort, and events will explain it.

8

Attack in the Air

It would not be surprising if the military aviation of those pioneer days were almost incomprehensible to pilots of World War II and even more so to flying students of the 1950s. Beside such a giant as the B-36 with its 230-foot wingspread and 47-foot tail, its speed of more than 435 miles an hour, its service ceiling of 45,000 feet, and its range of 10,000 miles, the Spads, DHs, Handley-Pages, Breguets, Nieuports, Fokkers, and Gothas of 1918 are like the frailest toys. In the pictures they look like boys' kites: in some ways they were built like kites. The wings were of cloth stretched over spruce spars. Wooden struts separated the wings of a biplane, and a lacing of steel wire ran between them. The pilot sat in the cockpit of the wood-and-fabric fuselage, exposed to the wind. A speed of 135 miles per hour was considered high, and few aircraft achieved an "endurance" of eight hours in the air. For pursuit planes two hours was the rule. Range was a few hundred miles. Ceilings were high, approaching 25,000 feet, providing a tough experience for the pilot. There was virtually no instrument panel, no radio communication between planes, no parachutes for the fliers. The landing gear again consisted of two wheels: take off and landing required no runway, only a fairly flat field.

We may imagine the effect of an incendiary bullet on such an inflammable "crate." More fliers were cremated in the air than were killed by crashes. Often these light machines would fall slowly to the ground and the pilot would survive, provided the craft did not catch fire. Forced landings were relatively easy. Many a German and Allied plane landed safely in a field behind the enemy's line when the fuel gave out or mechanical trouble developed. There was a camaraderie among airmen even when they were war enemies, and aviator prisoners were treated with special respect. Wounded Allied fliers were often cared for by the greatest German surgeons: there were cases of brilliant plastic surgery (at which the Germans were expert) performed in German hospitals over long periods of time on American aviators. World War I was still, in certain phases, a "gentleman's war."

Mitchell's diary for February, 1918, gives a sharp picture of the tricky flying of those days and, incidentally, of his own sporting, air-hunting impulses.

I have an excellent new Spad, single seater. The day after I got it a German Rumpler, as usual, started over our area. I happened to be on the airdrome when it was sighted, up about 15,000 feet, and I thought I would try to get up to it. . . . I started off in my Spad with all speed, taxied across the airdrome so as to turn it into the wind and then gave her the gun, that is, without bringing the ship to a full stop. If I cut the throttle and lost speed, the ship would undoubtedly turn over as the wings had already begun to lift so I gave it all the gas I had and just as I was leaving the ground I could hear what I thought was one of the wheels break. I never saw the German

Rumpler again, so after having climbed to about 12,000 feet, getting well chilled . . . I returned to the airdrome.

I could see officers and men bustling about in a great state of excitement as they saw my wheel had broken. . . . I . . . landed with great caution and put the weight of the ship on the right wheel because the left was broken. . . . Everyone was surprised that I had not turned over. The wheel, instead of collapsing sideways, had the spokes driven straight through the tires and in this way gave me considerable support.

Such an exploit by a commanding officer, who was supposed to play safe with his precious body, was certain to endear him to his command. Mitchell, in his thirty-ninth year, was an "old man" to most of the combat fliers. In addition he was a staff officer, usually associated with maps and conferences rather than with one-seater Spads on wild-goose chases into the sky "for fun." If officers of his rank and position flew at all, it was as a passenger in a two-seater observation plane.

But these things, which he was always doing, balanced certain traits likely to inspire criticism. As Clinton Gilbert wrote:

While his brother officers, the earth-borne commanders of the trenches, were plodding about in Dodges or what not, Mitchell was tearing along the roads twice as fast as they in his powerful racer. . . . He swaggered in an extraordinary uniform with marvelous patch pockets and unusual "pink pants," for his fancy has free rein in everything that adds a touch of the picturesque to his person. But perhaps the greatest outrage of all was his putting on his sleeve one more gold chevron for longer service than anyone else was entitled to.

Seeing him, however, in the sky with a broken wheel, watching him again and again experiment with a tough assignment before he ordered another to undertake it, watching his frequent, surprising tolerance of mistakes, many forgave the rest, and in time he came to be liked even for his "good theater."

In the early spring of 1918 the Allied position on the ground became desperate. In a smashing advance through the British Fifth Army, the Germans arrived almost at the gates of Paris. It was a time as perilous, as apparently hopeless, as the first September of the war, when French soldiers had driven out from Paris in taxis to reinforce the stand at the Marne. Another battle of the Marne was imminent, its outcome uncertain. Pershing was offering everything he had, trained or untrained, to the new generalissimo, Marshal Foch. Enormous contingents of American doughboys who scarcely knew how to shoot a rifle were arriving daily. But not a single American airplane had arrived.

Mitchell tempered his anger and impatience at this time with hard work, organizing his fliers into squadrons, experimenting with formations, carrying out maneuvers— always with French aircraft. Here again we see that the American effort was one of men, not machines. The skill these boys learned in the waiting interval was to pay off later regardless of American factory production. They were a gay lot, drinking and making merry in the uncertainty of each tomorrow, but they were earnest in the air.

Mitchell also satisfied his itch to know what the score was by lonely flights. In March he flew to Paris in his Spad and lost his way, finding himself at last over Soissons with only five minutes of gas left.

Soon I would have to land, out of gas in German territory. I turned around and flew till my gas gave out. I then turned on the emergency tank and landed in a field about twenty kilometers from Paris.

After that he flew over the German troops behind St. Quentin and watched the devastating offensive from the air. "The hole in the British Army," he recorded, "is twenty or thirty miles broad." He realized then, to the full, the power for defense that could be gained from thoughtful, interpretive air observation—a vision which he was to put to effective use in the last great battles of the war.

In April two American "pursuit" pilots won a victory in the air, which delighted Mitchell because of the large audience. He got a signal from an advance outpost that German planes were crossing our lines. He ordered three alerted pilots at the Toul airdrome to take the air. One failed to take off, but Lieutenants Douglas Campbell and Allan Winslow climbed into the fog which hid the Germans although "the whir of the German motors could be heard by the citizens of Toul."

All over the city, people stood still in the streets looking into the sky to see what *les Américains* would do. Fortunately the "Boche" planes came out of the fog in time for the full show to be visible to everyone. The Americans knocked them out of the air and returned unscratched to the airdrome in four and a half minutes. Apparently the German planes fell slowly, for the pilots were not killed and had stories to tell about the reasons for their flight. Mitchell did not believe them. He had his own theory.

The Germans knew full well that our air units had just reached the line. In all probability our men, new at the game, might not be as alert or as competent as they would be at a later date. Some German machines near this area had recently come right down on to the French airdrome at Toul, set fire with their flaming bullets to some French airplanes on the ground, and had shot up the whole place. . . .

If they could do this to the Americans right off the handle, it would have a dampening effect on our morale and would greatly increase that of the German Aviation. I have always thought that, taking advantage of the fog on that day, these German airplanes were attempting to do that very thing.

The shattered German planes were immediately put on exhibition in a square in Toul.

"The enthusiasm of the citizens was tremendous. I lost no time in publishing these facts all over the Army. . . ."

This insistence on quick publicity was characteristic. Mitchell never forgot the value of good news. This story of the four-and-a-half minute knockout of the "Boche" planes spread like fire not only through our own Army but through the ranks of the desperate French troops as well.

Little incidents of this kind had a remarkable psychological effect when the balance hung so delicately. Even a whispered rumor would embolden exhausted men to stand another day with their backs to the wall. We know now, of course, that the enemy, too, in spite of his spring victories was close to the end of his rope. The morale of German soldiers had been undermined by hunger, by conditions at home, and by insidious revolutionary propaganda which had infiltrated from Russia. Even some of the mistakes and ignorances of the green Americans scared the Germans. General Ludendorff wrote, after the war, that there was fear in the high command because Americans ignored camouflage and a belief that any fighting force

which exposed itself so recklessly to enemy air reconnaissance must have uncounted millions of reserves!

In May, about a month after this thrilling first American
show in the air, Mitchell suffered a series of personal blows
which would remain long in his memory. A less resilient
man with a less vigorous and constantly active mind might
have been shocked by these things into a numbness that
would have dulled his powers. Yet it is true that war, in
spite of all its horror or perhaps because this horror is so
universal, takes the sharp edge off personal tragedy. An
officer has such heavy responsibility toward his command
as a whole, such incessant demands for quick, detailed, and
technical thinking—so much to do, in short, that cannot
be delayed—that he has no time to dwell, as he would in
peacetime, on private disaster. And, in that infancy of aviation, an officer in Mitchell's spot had no book, no rules to
go by: he must originate or create a dozen new moves
every day. These are some of the reasons that Billy Mitchell
showed so little of the pain he must have suffered and
never for an instant lost the gaiety of his manner or the
firmness of his hand on all the controls.

On May 19 Mitchell was called by telephone to a little
village some 6 miles from his Toul headquarters. There, in
the back yard of a shoemaker's cottage, lay a body. A
sixteen-year-old girl was covering it with flowers. A few
minutes before, the body had fallen directly into the yard
among masses of flowering shrubs and fruit trees in bloom.
The girl had recognized the face, for it was known all
over that part of France. Raoul Lufbery was a special hero
to these people because, though he was an American
whose father was a citizen of the United States, his mother

had been a French peasant and Raoul's childhood had been lived in France.

Major Lufbery was a top ace. He had been a pursuit pilot in the Escadrille Lafayette for a year before the United States entered the war and had been credited with seventeen enemy planes, though everyone knew he had brought down twice that number. He was one of Billy Mitchell's closest friends.

The shoemaker told Mitchell the story. A German plane had come over, the alarm had sounded, the people had run for the cellars. Then someone had heard Lufbery's machine rising to intercept, and the people had cried, "The Americans are coming! We will be saved!" and had run out of the cellars to see the show. Suddenly the American plane turned upside down and what looked like a sack fell out of it.

I think it quite probable [Mitchell wrote in his diary] that Lufbery, in his hurry to get after the German plane, failed to tie himself in the plane with his belt; that the German shots cut his controls, his airplane turned over, and Lufbery fell out. Just think—if he had had a parachute he could easily have been saved!

Eight days later, while Mitchell was having lunch in a Toul café his adjutant came in, called Mitchell aside, and said, "I have some bad news for you. Your brother has crashed——"

"Is he dead?"

"Yes."

It was his younger brother, John, named for his father. He was fifteen years younger, and the difference made an unusual relationship between them, giving Billy a sense of responsibility toward him. Yet Billy had gone more than halfway to meet the boy's ambitions, his enthusiasm, and his fun, never insisting on a stuffy respect. Nor was John ever overawed by his brother's exalted position. He had tried to follow where Billy led, to emulate him, not because of hero worship, but because he believed in his brother's way and perhaps partly because he would not be left behind, straggling in the rear of the march of so distinguished a family.

At thirteen he had followed his captain-brother through several days of maneuvers in a private's uniform that Billy had got an army tailor to cut for him. Some nine years later he got himself into aviation "by stretching matters," as his brother wrote in his diary, "in his anxiety to be in the Air Service and be near me." Once he was there, however, a lieutenant serving with Colonel Mitchell, he was not above playing tricks on his magnificent brother. In the week before his death he had "borrowed" the colonel's racing Mercedes for a two-day trip to Paris without permission.

The full measure of Billy Mitchell's feeling is revealed in a letter to his mother a while after John's death. Here is the tenderness, the capacity for deep emotion, so seldom understood by those who called him "arrogant," "self-centered," or "hard-boiled."

John's loss [he wrote on June 26, 1918] I suppose was the hardest thing that ever happened to me. To begin with he was my only brother, he was so much younger that he was like a son, and in addition he was the same as a great friend. He had every quality that I wanted in a brother and admired in a man. I suppose he was very nearly the dearest living thing in the world to me. There is little use in talking about it because it is all over. I always thought that I would go first. . . . I think about you, I suppose, every hour of every day and I know what it means to you to have John gone, and just how calmly you are taking it outwardly and how deeply you feel inwardly. You can be sure of one thing. No mother could be prouder of a son than you can be of John. His grave is about four kilometers north of Toul, in the Sevastopol hospital cemetery. He lies among many comrades and friends. I have employed a farmer to keep growing flowers on it always and his squadron, the 1st Aero, put a large everlasting wreath with purple flowers and green leaves which is beautiful. . . .

One sentence, "There is little use in talking about it because it is all over," gives the key to Mitchell's habit of mind. His thought turned instantly from the past to the future. John is dead: other men are alive; we must do what we can to protect them. In his diary, immediately after, he wrote, "I have made up my mind more than ever to rely on the judgment of the doctors as to a man's fitness to fly."

Within the hour after the grave was filled, Colonel Mitchell was high in the air on one of his lonely inspection flights.

The two catastrophes coming so close together were disheartening enough, but in that same month another blow came from the rear. It was not death this time but a shock to pride and confidence which must have appeared unfair to himself and damaging to his work.

A picturesque hint of trouble to come is in the April section of the diary:

The General Staff is now trying to run the Air Service with just as much knowledge of it as a hog knows about skating. It is terrible to have to fight with an organization of this kind, instead of devoting all our attention to the powerful enemy on our front.

I have had many talks with General Pershing . . . some of them very heated, with much pounding on the table on both sides. One time he told me that if I kept insisting that the organization of the Air Service be changed he would send me home. I answered that if he did he would soon come after me. This made him laugh and our talk ended admirably.

To make "Black Jack" Pershing laugh when he was in one of his table-pounding moods was something few of his subordinates were able to do. Apparently, however, after Mitchell left, taking his peculiar charm with him, Pershing did not go on laughing. The more he thought about the Air Service, the more convinced he became that it should be run, like any other branch of the Army, by a West Point general who had proved himself efficient in other fields. It didn't matter in the least whether he knew how to fly or had the faintest understanding of aircraft. The fact that Pershing later learned that he was dealing with a wholly new and revolutionary weapon and that he made full amends for his earlier ignorance is as much to his credit as anything he did in the war.

Late in May he sent for a West Point classmate, General Mason Patrick, an engineer who was engaged in large construction work on docks, hospitals, cantonments, and railroads in the rear, and told him he had been appointed Commander of the entire Air Service.

"I have never in my life," wrote General Patrick, "been so surprised."

He told Pershing of his total ignorance of the subject, but Pershing shook his head. Patrick asked how it would be if he just handled administration and left the actual air command to someone else. Pershing said, "No"; he wanted one man on whom he could pin full responsibility.

The American Expeditionary Force was organized at that time in armies made up of army corps. This was still on paper only, but officers had been appointed to head these units. The upshot of Pershing's new order was that Mitchell was relieved as Chief of Air Service, First Army, by General Foulois and given the lower position of Chief of Air Service, First Army Corps, under Foulois's command. Pershing and Patrick seem to have arranged this transfer between them.

No one knows what goes on in the mysterious shadows of a staff headquarters. Officers in the field simply get their orders and obey them. Their inner feelings, when they are supplanted in the midst of their plans by outsiders who have had no part in these tremendous efforts, must be kept to themselves. Foulois, though a flier, had done much of his work in this war in the rear.

If Mitchell was bitter about these changes, we have no record of it. What he did was more intelligent than expressing hurt feelings. He submitted a scheme of organization to his new superior. He proposed putting all available planes and airmen into a brigade which he would command in immediate active work over the front. Additional brigades would be organized later as units became available, all to be under Foulois. To this General Foulois agreed, and Mitchell took his brigade to the front over Château-Thierry, where all hell was breaking loose.

It was July. Somewhere in the grim last days of that month or early in August came, according to historians on both sides, the turning point of the war. Ludendorff puts it precisely at the eighth of August. It is doubtful if the full effect of the Allied air forces in that turning of the tide has ever been adequately evaluated.

We know that the performance of our air armada took on an entirely new aspect. From the sensational but sporadic attacks of our planes, the heroic but unplanned dogfights, hit-or-miss bombings, and every sort of wild exploit, there came a sudden order and pattern in the skies. Aircraft flying in Vs with coordinated teamwork rose in what the frightened Germans called "masses hitherto unknown." We may believe it was the concentration and the purposeful order of these planes which made them think the quantity was so great.

We know, too, that for the first time British, French, and American squadrons were working in effective concert. This was Mitchell's idea; yet even he had not been sure that it would achieve success so quickly.

I never imagined [he wrote] that allies belonging to different nations could work together the way we did in the Air Force. It is impossible with ground troops. With us in the air we were all striving to perfect and develop a new power that the world had never seen before, which calls for qualities that are entirely different from those on the ground, and we therefore were all more or less on an even footing.

Looking back at this time, it seems as if a race of supermen had been born—above the obstacles of language because they had a common language of their own; above national animosities because, in a very literal sense, they were above frontiers, because they had two common enemies—the Germans and the element they flew in—and because they flew together into a future that had no connection with any past in the history of mankind.

At the start of the July battles (on the fourteenth) Mitchell flew alone and unprotected over the whole front. On the German side he was surprised by the color of the roads below; they were no longer white streaks but a grayish green. Dropping closer, he saw that the color came from the masses of German troops moving in unbroken lines against our forces. Flying back and forth, he found that these soldiers were headed toward five bridges across the Marne. He returned and reported the location of the bridges to the headquarters of Marshal Foch, with the result that the Allied armies knew the precise points at which to meet the assault.

The news of this flight and of Mitchell's subsequent handling of his brigade was a matter of general knowledge at American headquarters before the end of July. What General Pershing said or thought we do not know. There was one conversation between Mitchell and Pershing during this time "in the garden" of Pershing's house. It is probable that Mitchell then presented the broad air plan for the rest of the war, the outline of which he had already made. Whether Pershing then talked things over with Foulois is in doubt. But there is no question that General Foulois wrote to Pershing on July 25, recommending that Mitchell replace him as Chief of Air Service, First Army. The letter contains nothing but praise.

I wish [Foulois wrote] to bring to your attention the most efficient service of Colonel Mitchell during the past month in the organization, battle training, general supervision, and guidance of the Air Service units which have been operating with the Franco-American troops in the Château-Thierry area. . . . I am glad to say that the technical and tactical supervision exercised over these units by Colonel Mitchell has resulted in a minimum loss of life, a maximum effective use of material available, and a high fighting spirit of morale. . . .

History tells us that the Germans had begun to think of suing for peace in August, 1918. There was, however, no evidence of this in the theaters of operations. On the contrary, just east of the Château-Thierry–Vesle sector the Germans had built up a formidable salient. Its point was at St. Mihiel. Before the August fight was over, Mitchell had worked out the air strategy against this bulge. It was to be the largest air operation ever attempted and probably the greatest single event in Mitchell's career.

9

Fifteen Hundred Crates

FEAR MADE UP most of the bomb load of military airplanes in 1918. Ground troops were often terrified by the mere presence of an enemy plane above them, even if it was un-armed. If it was an observation plane, it could take news of the troops' location to the enemy's artillery. If it car-ried the extremely light bombs that were possible for such aircraft, infantrymen were far more afraid of them than of more accurately fired and more destructive artillery shells. There seemed to be no way of taking cover from a sky weapon. You could guess roughly about the area that would be covered by gunfire, but no one knew where the bombs from a plane would land.

Much of the terror came from ignorance. The training—of American troops especially—had contained very little about aviation. The whole thing was new, misunderstood, and had a suggestion of the superhuman about it. Fear of an air raid was something like the fear of a storm or an earthquake. The American soldiers had little faith that their own air force could do anything about it. This was one of the things that griped Billy Mitchell.

It is practically impossible [his diary notes] to impress the men in the ranks, through their own officers, as to the value of aviation. They do not even know what the insignia of our planes is in many cases.

He tells stories of high-ranking American officers taking shelter at the approach of Allied planes. He writes repeatedly about ground officers failing to cooperate with the air force, of not giving pilots and observers the proper signals, the necessary information to help them in their work against the enemy.

All this, of course, was quite natural. There had been little in the training or education of company, battalion, or even division commanders that had to do with this strange new weapon. West Pointers knew that cavalry, artillery, and engineers had to work together, keep information flowing from one branch to another, and that success depended on their scheduled coordination. But they had only the vaguest idea how this new arm could cooperate with the group. The notion persisted that it was a sort of maverick, or lonely outfit, only occasionally visible, engaged in wild hit-or-miss adventures in high and distant points. It must be admitted that the American aviators, at least up to Château-Thierry, had done little to change this view. A few wiser tacticians in the upper echelons saw the air force as a supercavalry, faster than the rest of the Army and so able to reconnoiter in the van. But there were men who had studied air power, not from the books where there was virtually nothing, but by watching it work.

Mitchell, however, was not so tolerant of this ignorance as a milder, more patient, and more reflective man might have been. He was so sure, himself, of what had to be

done, so concentrated on the large plan that was forming
in his mind, and so aware of how little time he had to put
it into practice that he seems sometimes to have got un-
duly angry at pardonable blindness.

In his impatience he hit suddenly on an idea. If the
officers could not instruct their men about the Air Service,
then the Air Service itself would take on the job. Mitchell
arranged for the printing of a great quantity of instruction
sheets addressed directly to the enlisted men in language
they could understand and had them dropped from planes
on encampments and troop concentrations everywhere. It
may not have been tactful to go over the heads of officers
in this way, but tact was not one of Billy Mitchell's out-
standing talents. We may suspect, however, that some of
the officers were grateful. The sheets were headed, "From
the American Scrappers in the Air to American Scrappers
on the Ground," and read:

DOUGHBOYS
While you are giving the Boche hell on the ground, we are
helping you to the limit in the air. . . .

Headquarters is trying to keep in touch with you and to render aid whenever you are checked or outnumbered.

Keep us posted at all times as to where your front lines are,
either with Bengal lights, panels, or—if nothing else is available—wave a white towel or any white cloth.

Your signals enable us:
To take news of your location to the rear.
To report if the attack is successful.
To call for help if needed.
To enable the artillery to put their shells over your head
into the enemy. . . .

Do not think that we are not on the job when you cannot see us—most of our planes work so far to the front that they cannot be seen from the lines.

Some of the enemy planes may break through our airplane barrage in front of you, and may sometimes bomb and machine-gun you, but in the last month we have dropped ten tons of bombs for every one the Boche has dropped. For every Boche plane that you see over you, the Boche sees ten Allied planes over him. . . .

After reading this, pass it on to your buddie.

It was the custom for the boys on the ground to surround a German plane which had crashed and tear it to pieces for souvenirs. Mitchell's scatter sheets said the Germans knew about this incorrigible American habit and often put booby traps in their planes to kill the souvenir hunters. They also told of the great value to our Intelligence of every part of a crashed enemy plane: its instruments, its controls, its motor, its markings.

After he had thus brought home the value of air power to the men in the mud, he tackled the somewhat more difficult job of making his plan for the complex St. Mihiel attack understood by staff officers.

"It is," he wrote in his diary early in September, "the greatest concentration of air power that has ever taken place."

His exuberance over the dramatic aspect of his concept was characteristic. Mitchell, the showman, always walked side by side with Mitchell, the strategic thinker and plan-ner.

It is the first time in history in which an air force, co-operating with an army, is to act according to a broad strategical plan, which contemplates not only facilitating the advance of the ground troops, but spreading fear and consternation into the enemy's line of communications, his replacement system, and the cities and towns behind them which supply our foe with the sinews of war.

The theory was not wholly original with Mitchell. We get a hint of this fact in the diary when, immediately after this quoted passage, he remembers General Trenchard, of the British air force. It was his long talks with Trenchard which started him thinking in the pattern he was to put into practice at St. Mihiel. Trenchard had seen the "broad strategical plan" as a theory early in the war. But he had been frustrated by the fact that the British air force had been under the stern command of the army, whereas his vision saw aviation as *cooperating* with the army, not bossed by it. It should have its independent staff of air experts, knowing precisely what the score was in the air, which would issue its own orders based on what was planned on the ground. But Trenchard, like Mitchell, was a man who, though an air expert, knew more about the ground than any of the ground staff knew about the air.

However old the theory might be, it was quite true, as Mitchell said, that there had been no practice of it on a large scale. Yet Mitchell's task in getting it off the blueprint and into the air was as delicate as Trenchard's had been. He had to convince the old-school line of officers of the Army that he could not take detailed orders from them but would work out his own line according to his view of what went on on the ground. He must, therefore, appeal to the wisdom of the wise ones and by-pass the stuffy "brass hats" who insisted on the rules in the book. Fortunately there were wise ones there.

General Pershing was like an intelligent coach who, rather than dictate all the plays of the game, is willing to leave many to a brilliant quarterback whom he can trust. Pershing had learned much; his table pounding had become more discreet. Here was support in the highest quarter. But Mitchell's greatest ally was General Hunter Liggett, commanding the First Army, a fine air enthusiast and a penetrating student of air techniques as well as a brilliant master of troop tactics, logistics, communications, and supply. And he had also the full sympathy of the air-minded French. So his plan was finally approved, book or no book.

The diary, starred by superlatives and sometimes lurid with adjectives, only touches lightly on the complicated details of preparation. He does remark that he got only three hours' sleep in each twenty-four. He read reports till 2 A.M. and was up at 5 A.M. to watch practice maneuvers. Major Harry Toulmin, however, who held the vague title of Air Force Coordinating Officer, gives us a picture of these in his history of the Air Service, AEF:

The preliminary preparation involved the elaborate construction of new airdromes. . . . [It must be remembered that the frail aircraft of the time required hangars.] It involved the assembly of squadrons from the whole Western Front which necessitated the transport of this equipment and the flying of their planes into this territory without attracting the attention of the enemy . . . the co-ordination of Air Service with the Army plans, and the provision of fuel, transport, ammunition and bombs in great quantities . . . the arrangement for large reserves of planes and spare parts . . . each airdrome and headquarters . . . interconnected by telephone, telegraph and wireless telegraphy . . . and a system of communication

between the units of the Air-Service and of the several staffs
. . . over these lines and by motorcycle, automobile and airplane. . . .

From his own team and from army engineers Mitchell
had magnificent assistance. His fighter patrols were constantly in the sky screening all this business from the enemy.
Some of the figures of this time, such as the great Frank
Luke, of Arizona, and his partner Joe Wehner, Eddie Rickenbacker, Harold Hartney, Elmer Haslett, and Lewis
Brereton, have gone down in history or on to brilliant
achievement in peace and in another war. But Mitchell
was always suspicious that a monkey wrench might suddenly get into the machinery of the rear which reeled red
tape as well as the smooth ribbon of grand strategy. And
sure enough, on the eve of the attack it was thrown in.

Through the day Mitchell had flown over the salient
with his close French friend, Paul Armengaud, in the ob-
server's seat. From the air an unexpected German movement was suddenly clear to them.

We know from history that the Germans, who had held
this salient since 1915, had decided in September, 1918,
that it was dangerous. They knew that it was surrounded
by Allied armies. Their confidence in holding strong points
had been weakened by the Allied victories of the summer.
They had, therefore, started an orderly retreat, knowing
that it was easier to hold a short, straight line than a long,
curving one. They believed they had plenty of time; they
were sure the Allies would not attack until the fifteenth
or later.

Mitchell and Armengaud saw the full proof of the retreat. They saw troops and supplies moving quietly along

the roads to the rear. What a chance to turn a retreat into a rout, to cut off the rear, to trap the whole body in the salient now before it had a chance to escape! The Allies had already planned a surprise attack. But what panic they could cause, springing it while the Germans had their backs turned! There was no time to be lost. And only the air force could do the necessary job on the back areas if it could start before the German airmen were alerted.

Mitchell rushed to Pershing's headquarters, where the general and his staff were meeting, and told his news. The "brass" looked at the impetuous colonel coldly.

"Pretty bad weather," said an engineer officer.

"What has the weather to do with it?" Mitchell asked.

"Well, rain always holds up our light railways that we use to get ammunition to our artillery. And that goes for water supply, too. It would be better to hold off for a few days."

Another and then another officer agreed. Mitchell could scarcely believe his ears.

"But we must jump the Germans now!" he said. "Now, in their retreat. I tell you I've seen their movement to the rear with my own eyes. Forget the artillery if it means delay. If we advance fast, the artillery would probably shoot a lot of our own men anyway."

Billy Mitchell knew that the effect of artillery would come from the sky, but he also knew how hard it was to convince these old-school ground officers of *that*.

Through the group, men were nodding their agreement with the engineer. Yes, yes, better wait. It would clear presently. Nothing would be lost.

Just men, Mitchell thought, just brave men would be

lost, his own men, his fliers. He knew what a powerful air force the enemy could send up if it were given time. Yet here in this group he was the junior member. The others all ranked him. How could he make his lone opinion prevail? There were some tense moments after he had spoken. Then suddenly Pershing looked across at him and smiled. It was one of his great moments—an instant of quick, quiet decision not unlike that in which he defied the generalissimo, Marshal Foch, himself.

"We will attack," he said, "without delay."

The curtain went up at dawn on September 12. This was three days ahead of the Germans' best guess about an Allied attack. The diary records that the day was "dark and cloudy with intermittent rain. Clouds hung low and the visibility was very poor. Nevertheless, our Air Service, with that of the Allies, went over the lines, and I was much pleased with the fact that virtually no German airplanes got over our ground troops."

The salient was shaped like a pointed horseshoe: on the map it looked like a carelessly drawn letter "V." Great bodies of Allied troops were drawn up along the sides hemming in the Germans so that their only movement could be to the rear unless they could break through our flanking forces. But Mitchell knew that if the enemy's air force could cross these flanks and break out of the V it could do serious damage to the rear of our troops, cutting off their supplies. His great effort was to keep every German plane inside the horseshoe, always over their own armies, never over ours.

He formed two attack brigades of some 400 planes each. One of them attacked the right side of the V, drawing all the German aviation there to defend the flank. This left the rear—the wide part of the V—defenseless, and to it Mitchell sent bombers to cut off the communications of the enemy troops in the salient. He then sent his second attack brigade to the left side of the salient while the first refueled, so that the enemy air force had to rush to that side. In this way he gave the German aviators no rest, no respite: kept them constantly within the salient with their rear forever open to the terrorizing bombing. This maneuver, coming as a total surprise with an organization that operated with clockwork precision and with quantities in the air without precedent in that infancy of sky warfare, gave a crushing blow from which even the valiant German enemy could never recover. It was not a physical blow as such things are reckoned in war. Casualties on both sides were surprisingly low. But morally it was a catastrophe. An army without a rear, cut off from its homeland, thwarted in both advance and retreat, and covered from above is an army lost indeed.

In two days 16,000 Germans surrendered. In two days the entire St. Mihiel salient was destroyed as an enemy strong point. After it, to rally their army for further attack was impossible for the Germans. From then on they were continuously on the defensive, grimly struggling to hold what they had against a million fresh American soldiers. That they kept their resistance tough to the end, no one who remembers the slow sweep through the Argonne Forest will ever forget. But new confidence had come to the exhausted French poilus and to the still-vigorous but bewildered Americans, and much of it, in those dark, wet fall days, came out of the sky.

On the first of October, Mitchell was promoted to brigadier general and put in command of the Air Service of the
Group of Armies. In mid-October, when no one believed
that less than a month of war was left, he talked again to
Pershing. He had a plan for the spring of 1919. It was so
fantastic that Pershing's acceptance of it as a definite
project to be carried out if the war continued proves his
confidence in this far-thinking air strategist.

The proposal was for air-borne troops. There were, at
the time, a few big Handley-Page machines capable of
transporting ten or fifteen men with their equipment, and
others were in production. By spring Mitchell thought we
could assemble a large fleet of such planes to fly over the
enemy's lines and drop men and machine guns by parachute in his rear.

That such a dream could have come true in those early
years of aviation is extremely doubtful. But it is an example
of Mitchell's kind of vision. While he worked with what
he had, he was always thinking in terms of what he would
have if aviation made logical progress. Sometimes it must
have seemed to him that the future was already in his
hands. That is why, even in 1918, he was able to accom-
plish what others thought impossible. His mind appeared
to be always stretching the power of the airplane, and because his will was so strong, he actually made it perform
what seemed to be miracles. Actually there was no miracle;
he simply saw power that was already there but was invisible to others. Like all pioneers, he would say, "We *ought*
to be able to do this or that. Let's try it!"

According to Henry H. ("Hap") Arnold, he did try the
parachute-attack idea after the war at Kelly Field, and it

worked in a carefully executed demonstration. Arnold wrote that "troops with machine guns could be and were landed by parachute" and that the men after landing were able to set up and operate their guns "in less than three minutes by actual test."

It was typical of Mitchell that he take the first opportunity of proving any theory he might hold. Yet, though it was said to be successful at Kelly Field in a planned show with no enemy present, we cannot be sure that it would have worked in a war. There were many elements involved. The scale would have to be large. Quantities of heavy planes would have to be produced in a hurry. And some of the disasters which actually attended some of our first air-borne operations in World War II lead us into doubt.

The great misfortune was, however, that the United States Army forgot the whole idea until, some twenty years later, it was taken by the Russians and made a commonplace operation in their army. And the Germans took it from them before we made a move. It was developed at last in American strategy under Mitchell's colleague Lewis Brereton.

In all the strenuous work that went into the Air Service's triumphs in September and October there were sure to be amusing side lights. One of them Mitchell recorded in a "dead-pan" manner in his diary. He was insistent that there should never be any fogginess in the mind of anyone who read or heard his orders. Crystal clarity—one-syllable clarity, if necessary—was the rule. He, therefore, kept close by his side at his headquarters an officer who was "not particularly bright," to whom he read everything before it was issued. If *he* could understand it, Mitchell was sure anyone could.

With the end of the war in November came also the end of a phase in Mitchell's life. For a year and a half he had brought all the power of his knowledge and experience as a soldier and a flier to combat the ignorance he had met at almost every turn. He had won through against maladministration and service jealousies to a pinnacle of command. He had gained the respect of British, French, and Italian allies. He had learned much from great air leaders, such as Trenchard, Armengaud, and Douhet, and had combined their teachings with his own vision in a new plan under which the Allies united in a startling victory. Most important, perhaps, of all, he had shown a power over men's loyalties which would endure throughout his life and, indeed, survive him.

If the war had continued, Billy Mitchell would have gone on, no doubt, to greater triumphs and might have established an American air force pattern in accord with his convictions. But with the war at an end he faced something very different. No longer was there a tangible enemy to unite the nation's armed forces. To take its place would come petty internal enmities, difficult to discern or understand, intolerable to a direct fighter of Mitchell's temper. Yet fight these things he must—or rather fight through them—to a new peacetime victory for air power. This was the next phase. Before he left Europe, he could already see the shapes of the enormous obstacles that loomed ahead.

Even while the spectacular air shows were going on over

France, a shadow had fallen on the Air Service at home. In the United States there had been a failure as surprising as the successes abroad. To determine and remove its cause, to prevent its reappearance became, now that the fight against the enemy in the sky was over, the dominating purpose of Mitchell's life.

10

"No More War"

THE "WAR TO END WAR" was over. The cry, "Get the boys
home!" rose from thousands of American homes. When the
"boys" came—as fast as transports could be found to carry
them—there were a few triumphant parades. Tons of ticker
tape and torn-up telephone books were showered on the
first heroes. But as the spring of 1919 wore on, the people
grew tired of celebrating, bored by the stories the "boys"
were telling and anxious to forget the things that had
strained their emotions for two years and get back to the
business of peace.

Billy Mitchell arrived in mid-February. He had spent
the months after the armistice in the army of occupation
in Germany. There was time there to think about the past
and the future. He was proud of the job the young fliers
had done under his command; yet he had tragic memories.
He could not forget something that, in the last weeks of
the war, became known all over the western front as a
"flaming coffin."

In contrast to the proud boasts that America would build
100,000 airplanes by the end of 1918, only 740 were at the
front at the armistice. Less than a third of these were ac-

tually used. None of them were combat planes. They were De Havilland 4s, two-seaters fit only for observation and photography. They were powered by Liberty motors. Their structure was too light for the engines. Worst of all, their unprotected fuel tanks were too close to the motors. If a bullet pierced the tank, the ship would catch fire. If the plane crashed, explosive fire was almost certain. Nine of Mitchell's men had been burned to death shortly before the end of the war. That such things should happen because of mechanical weakness in a machine produced by the world's greatest industrial nation was galling to a patriotic American. That his country had fallen down so completely on airplane production that his fliers had been forced to rely entirely on French, British, or Italian aircraft was something Billy Mitchell never forgot.

Still he had high hopes for the future. The failure would make the needs clear. America, first in the air, must redeem the strange breakdown and build a great air force. By the time he came home, it had become Mitchell's mission to make this dream come true. From here on to the end of his life he was a crusader. That is what we remember, and perhaps, always will. The incidents of his life may be forgotten. The revolution that followed his crusade is as vital a turning point as any in American history.

The harbor whistles blew as the *Aquitania* passed the Narrows. On board was a new kind of general. Field commanders, staff strategists who had moved their bodies of fighters over the enemy's trenches, were an old story. But there was something mysterious about a general of the air. What had he actually done up there in the clouds with those terrifying little machines? No one knew precisely.

Old men felt uncertain, insecure, as this herald of a new world came among them; boys were tense in the half-consciousness that he held their own futures in his hardy hands.

It was a noisy hero's welcome—noise was the fashion in those early days of peace—but the echo of it faded fast. Back in the American peacetime Army the show was over; there were no more heroics. As officers settled into garrison routine, paper work, close-order drill, and maneuvers that seemed meaningless now that the curtain was down on real war, there was time for "spit and polish," heel clicking, and the old jealousies. Officers who since 1917 had fought the battles of Washington, Camp Dix, and the California Presidio looked with green eyes on the "battle-scarred veterans" who had made the headlines. But the sourest looks of all were exchanged between those who had flown and those who had struggled in the mud. Who were these upstarts—undisciplined "lone eagles" forever escaping from the rugged march, the dirty trench, getting their "three squares" a day, and sleeping at night in a bed with sheets? And the answer: What can a "dog face" know of real adventure, of shooting when you are upside down at a wild, diving target 10,000 feet above your solid ground, of being faced with a choice of death by jumping or burning?

Old Academy men, graduates from West Point and Annapolis, were inclined in those days to be afraid of new ideas. Some of them still thought in terms of Indian fighting or galloping against Filipinos. The war, to be sure, had jolted them for the moment out of this kind of thinking, but they settled back into it when peace came. They loved the smell of horses or gunpowder, the sound of bugles, the thrill of scouting patrols. The new machines worried them.

General Milling, one of the great pioneer fliers, once said a pointed thing about the officers of the old services: "Their minds went only as far as their men could go. The infantry officer's horizon was at the end of a day's march. The cavalryman saw a little further, a little faster. The artillery-man could see to the end of his trajectories. But none of them could see into the air."

There were, however, brilliant exceptions. Hunter Liggett was one. The colonel, trained in the infantry, who became General "Hap" Arnold was another. And there were those in the Navy—Admirals Sims, Winterhalter, and Fullam—who saw far beyond the day's knots of ships.

The first acts of Billy Mitchell's crusade alarmed the Army and set the old school against him. But even as he landed, there was a plan in his mind which two years later was to scare the Navy almost out of its wits. He talked about this along with many other unpleasant things in the spring of 1919.

It has been said that he talked too much, too loud. That a gentler, more diplomatic approach would have been more effective. But these things were not in his character. He loathed gumshoe tactics: pulling wires off stage, soft words, anything that smelled of hypocrisy. The truth was too clear to him to allow any beating about the bush. Years later, in a letter to a friend, he remembered this time bitterly.

After the World War, [he wrote] having commanded the or-ganization that I did, to enter a life of political intrigue and four-flushing, where the person with the most glib tongue and softest handshake could get away with things he had not the courage to do against the enemy or the ability to devise in time of peace, was not to my liking, nor to that of the men around me.

In his mind there was no middle ground between blunt telling of the truth and "four-flushing." His enemies called him a "self-centered, ambitious politician." He was anything but. Any politician who used Mitchell's hammer-and-tongs method would soon be looking for another job.

The idea which had crystallized in Mitchell's mind was a plan which would put future American aviation into the hands of those who understood it. By understanding it, he meant not only knowing how to fly, knowing the mechanics of airplanes, their design, and power plants but seeing aviation as a new force in the world both in war and in peace to which the old forces would have to adjust.

In April, 1919, he told his idea to the Navy. It had asked him to talk to the high Navy Board, expecting him to tell what a fine "adjunct" to the Navy airplanes could be. It expected him to show how nicely aviation could be made to fit into the noble old scheme of sea power.

But General Mitchell was not thinking about what it would expect. He was not in the least awed by the gold braid. This was no special virtue of Billy Mitchell. He was simply too concentrated on his idea, too busy with his own thought, too far in the future to be awed by the past or intimidated by the present. When he spoke, he looked forward, further than the binoculars of the admirals could see. When he looked forward, he saw an event that would take place eleven years after his death.

"If we look forward," he said, "there will be a ministry of defense, combining Army, Navy, and air force under one direction."

He meant, as he explained then and continued to explain until 1936, that the air force should be wholly separate from Army and Navy, under its own head who would be accountable directly to an over-all secretary of national defense. Detachments of such an air force could and should be sent to the aid of both Army and Navy. But the war had proved that, in this new world, there were things an air force could do in war that neither Army nor Navy could possibly do. Brand-new techniques and machinery and a wholly new kind of strategy were required.

It took disasters at Pearl Harbor and the Philippines in 1941, many later painful lessons administered to Americans by Germans and Japanese, and two years of angry post-war discussion to persuade the old departments that Billy Mitchell had been right in 1919. The National Security Act of 1947 provided the plan he had "looked forward" to see while the myopic admirals on the board strained their eyes and then shook their heads.

What, they asked him, could an air force do on its own that armies and navies could not do? It could fly, he told them, over factories far in the rear beyond the reach of guns—factories where war materials were being made—and destroy them. It could smash roads and railroads in the very heart of an enemy nation. It could do these things in the first days of the war before the armies could mobilize. And it could destroy an invading enemy navy off the coast.

"It could do *what?*"

We may imagine the old sea dogs leaning forward with their hands behind their ears to make sure they had heard.

"Bomb ships. Sink them."

"Battleships?"

"Yes."

It seems incredible today that sane men, decorated with the world's highest honors, revered for their knowledge and understanding of war, could have asked these questions and disbelieved the answers.

But there was one—there may have been more who thought it wiser not to speak—who took the risk and said, "Yes," he believed young Mitchell spoke the truth, even about ships.

"They are most vulnerable," said Admiral Winterhalter, "to attack from the air. . . . There isn't anything that has appeared to me more important than cooperation in this new service. The need is imperative. . . . Unless it is solved, we shall surely go to pieces."

There was always someone like Winterhalter. Mitchell did not have, as has been said, to "go it alone." But behind the Winterhalters there was always someone else, more powerful, standing in a shadowy background, who could ring down the curtain when the Winterhalters and the Mitchells, the Simses and the Fullams, the Arnolds and the Liggetts started to speak.

So the members of the board bowed Mitchell out and shut the door behind him. What the other admirals said to Winterhalter is not on record.

While this was going on in the Navy, the Secretary of War was beginning to worry. The people of the country and the Congress representing them were not at all happy about the recent American performance in the air over France. It kept them from forgetting the war. Something had gone very badly wrong, dimming the victory. The

Senate had already begun an inquiry asking why it had cost a billion dollars to produce a handful of "flaming coffins." Secretary Baker wanted the people to know that he, too, was trying to get at the bottom of the whole aviation muddle and set up a new program for the Army based on the best available knowledge. He appointed a commission. At its head he put Assistant Secretary of War Benedict Crowell, who then chose three aircraft manufacturers, a Navy captain, and two Army colonels.

Baker told Crowell to make a study under three headings —organization, technical development, and commercial development—and to turn in a report. He then made what he found out later to have been a mistake from his point of view. He sent the commission to Europe.

Crowell and his men came home some two months later and handed the Secretary of War a report dated July 19, 1919. Mr. Baker read the report and filed it. As the summer wore on into fall and the fall into winter, several people began to wonder why the report had not been published.

One of those who wondered about this was a fiery little man of Italian descent who sat, at the time, in the Congress as a Representative from New York. He was an air enthusiast. He had been an Air Service officer on the Italian front. One of the great airports of the world has been named for him. His name was Fiorello H. La Guardia.

Mr. La Guardia made something of a nuisance of himself on the subject of the Crowell mission and its report. Finally he was appointed chairman of a subcommittee on aviation of the House Committee on Military Affairs. This Committee on Military Affairs and a similar one in the

Senate have always been and perhaps always will be thorns in the flesh of the War Department.

La Guardia opened hearings on December 4 and invited Mr. Crowell to testify. The report came out then and was spread on the record. Also revealed was the reason, as the next day's newspapers eagerly explained, for its remaining in the War Department's files since mid-July. The Secretary of War, Mr. Baker stated in a note appended to the report, had disagreed with its conclusions. What, asked La Guardia, did the report recommend?

"It recommended," Mr. Crowell replied, "the concentration of the air activities of the United States—military, naval, and civilian—within the scope of a single government agency created for the purpose, coequal in importance with the Departments of War, Navy, and Commerce."

Here was something that was even a jump ahead of Billy Mitchell! But Mitchell had not thought it necessary to go into the civilian aspects. That would come later. Divorce of Air Service from Army and Navy was the first step, and that was favored from beginning to end of the Crowell report.

And how, Chairman La Guardia asked, had Crowell's group come to its conclusions?

Separately, Crowell told him. Each man had gone on his own private investigation, interviewing men in the high echelons of army and navy in England, France, and Italy. When they got together to compare notes, the members of the commission found they agreed completely.

As evidence of British opinion, Crowell quoted from a speech by Lord Fisher, First Sea Lord of the Admiralty:

By land and by sea the approaching aircraft development knocks out the present fleet, makes invasion practicable, cancels our being an island, transforms the atmosphere into a battle-ground of the future. There is only one thing to do with the ostriches who are spending these vast millions on what is as useful for the next war as bows and arrows. Sack the lot. As the locusts swarmed over Egypt, so will aircraft swarm in the heavens, carrying inconceivable cargoes of men and bombs some fast and some slow. Some will act like battle cruisers and others as destroyers. All cheap—and this is the gist of it—re-quiring only a few men as crew.

A reflection of this last paragraph appeared more than twenty years later when Winston Churchill spoke of the Royal Air Force's defense of Britain in a broadcast on July 14, 1940: "Never in the field of human conflict was so much owed by so many to so few."

The La Guardia hearings went on for two months. They brought out every detail of the commission's work and went on to the testimony of fliers and military men on the desira-bility of an independent and united air force. Mitchell spoke his piece again and again. But when the hearings closed in February, nothing was done.

It was too late. Already the Army had reduced its Air Service, the Navy had abolished its Air Division. Admiral William S. Benson was shouting, "Aviation is just a lot of noise." Pershing, returning from Europe amid accolades, had announced, to Mitchell's great disappointment, that he was opposed to a separate air force.

Yet the hearings of the La Guardia committee were of immense importance. A seed was planted then that was never let die. They were the first guns of a battle that would last through World War II to 1947. They alerted

Congress, which never again slept when the air was talked about. More immediately, they introduced Billy Mitchell to Congress, and Congress became his ally two years later when the Navy tried to frustrate the bombing tests in Chesapeake Bay.

In these first postwar years Mitchell was far from down-hearted or discouraged despite his disillusionment. He worked long hours as Assistant Chief of Air Service under General Mason Patrick. He became interested in civil aviation and laid out airways over the nation which were later used by commercial air transport.

By the middle of 1920 he was aware that the War and Navy Departments and the old line officers were enemies. His testimony before Congress had been far more disturbing to them than anything he had said in private to the Navy Board. He was a picturesque and spectacular figure, and newspaper editors hung on his words and printed thousands of them. From printing his photographs they went on to print cartoons unfavorable to the services with Mitchell as the central figure. He was not, of course, responsible for these, but word was passed around that he was "going over the heads" of his superiors to the people.

Early in 1921, after much public agitation and a congressional resolution, the Joint Army and Navy Board agreed to permit the bombing of certain captured German ships by the Army Air Service. Though the Navy had opposed these maneuvers from the time he had first suggested them, many admirals, after the tests were scheduled, took comfort in the certainty that the attempt would be a sensational failure and that that would be the end of Billy Mitchell.

He was not disturbed by these attitudes and guesses, but he was determined, not only that the bombing should not be a failure, but that it should be as spectacular a success as any he had ever achieved. He knew well enough that you could not simply go out some nice day with a fleet of planes and casually sink ships. He knew that fliers who had never before attempted such a thing required long, constant practice, a rigorous period of training. Through the spring of 1921 he organized his Provisional Air Brigade at Langley Field and, day after day, bombed targets.

In this command he maintained as thorough a "spit-and-polish" regime as that of any field officer. Everything must be cleaned and shined, machines in perfect order, quarters immaculate, and uniforms without a tear, a spot, or a hole. On Saturdays he would put on a full-scale formal inspection with drill, bands playing, bugles blowing, and, showman that he always was, he invited crowds to come and watch. Then, in his most flaring blouse with pink breeches, always carrying his thin cane, he passed among his men, never missing a wrong trick.

In his private life, as that year wore on, there was a shadow. According to one of his biographers, Mr. Isaac Don Levine, Mitchell's long absence abroad had "caused a breach" with his wife which was widened by "his status as a social lion" on his return and "his zeal in the crusade for air power." Even the birth of a son, named John after his dead brother, in 1920 and his attachment to their two daughters, Harriet and Elizabeth, had failed to mend the break. Mitchell's only reference to her in his 1921 diary was the brief statement that she had left for Europe in March and returned in May. They were divorced in 1922.

We have come to the event with which this book began. There are many Americans who know little or have not heard of Billy Mitchell's performance in World War I. But there can be very few who have heard his name who do not know something of the bombing of the ships in Chesapeake Bay.

11

Honeymoon in the East

A GLANCE AT THE DIARY for 1921 shows how little time was left from Mitchell's duties and strenuous recreation for worry about private trouble or official opposition.

January 3. Flew.
4. Testified House Appropriations Committee. Dinner Alfalfa Club.
5. Flew S-E 5 Bolling Field.
6. Flew S-E 5 and De Havilland to Great Falls. Tested Thompson machine gun.
13. Went to Nott's Island, hunted quail. Looked over ground for airdrome sites.
14. Hunted ducks and geese on Currituck Sound.
February 3. Flew to Quantico, Va., and back to Washington.
4–8. Testified before House Naval Affairs Committee.
12. As acting Chief of Air Service presided over ceremonies of dedication of airway between Washington and Bolling Field. Boy Scouts laid cornerstones.
15. Dinner at City Club, talk to Boy Scouts.
17. Wrote article for *World's Work*.
19. Dinner and dance at Langley Field Clubhouse.
March 10. Flew to Aberdeen to witness dropping of bombs.
17. Flying time for day 6 h 35 m.

21–23. Witnessed bombing tests.
  31. Took Martin bomber up in the air at Langley Field
      for 2¼ hours. Bombarded battleship target. Flew
      out over mouth of the bay and around Chesapeake
      Bay. Took Captain's gig out and observed bomb-
      ing from surface of water. [This and most of the
      other practice was done with dummy bombs, sand
      or concrete, of the proper weight.]
April 4. Flew to Newport, R.I., 1 h 10 m.
  7–8. At Mitchell Field. [The diary does not say that on
      the night of April 7, the General attended the
      "Aviator's Ball" at the Waldorf in New York. Other
      records state that he flew to New York for this pur-
      pose. But Billy Mitchell always combined busi-
      ness and pleasure. He spent the day of the seventh
      inspecting the New York air base and the night
      dancing.]
  9. N.Y. to Washington, 2½ hrs heavy storms. [This
      was his return trip after the ball.]
  19. Bombing practice at Aberdeen.
  24. Rode horseback and played tennis.
May 16–19. Attended horse show. Took 2 seconds with [his
      horse] "Home Again."

In all this time of preparation for the big July show,
Mitchell followed every detail of the bombing practice personally. He was not content with the reports of subordinates, however much he trusted them, about what, for example, a Martin bomber could do over the water. At the
same time he was doing a routine job in the Washington
office of the Air Service, where maps were being made for
airways for eventual commercial air transport over the
country.

Men are worn out by work like this because they concentrate too steadily. Mitchell was able to shift his concentration. This is the happy talent that keeps a man healthy no matter what his burdens. To arrange your time so that from nine to ten o'clock you are completely focused on one job, from ten to eleven you do something wholly different, and at eleven can come back again, without missing a beat, to the first task takes a peculiar kind of mind.

We may imagine Billy Mitchell on a slack morning when he would have to wait till the next day for a report or an order to go on with what he was doing. He did not put his feet on the desk, light a pipe, and go on thinking about his work, worrying, guessing, or regretting. He did not pace up and down the room, snapping his fingers, scolding his secretaries, telephoning a dozen people, working himself into an exhausting fever of impatience because of a delay. He would look out the window and say:

"What a day for shooting!"

"How about a couple of hours in the air? The visibility is good. I might see something important."

"That horse is eating his head off in the stable. A few hours hard riding will get him in shape. Or maybe he needs some schooling for the show."

"Here's a chance to finish that article I promised the *Review of Reviews*—until the rain lets up."

Or he would write letters. Somehow, even in the busiest times, his wide correspondence never fell behind. Many of these letters have been preserved. There is hardly a case of even trivial notes to him going unanswered for more than a week. He wrote his father about politics, his mother about his adventures, his sisters about every sort of personal interest. He wrote constantly to newspaper editors, flying friends, horse dealers and trainers, scientists, inventors; to his "fans" and to his critics. To his colleagues, Army officers, "men of few words," who often had to spend half an hour phrasing a sentence, he was a source of amazement.

When the bombing was over in July, Mitchell, in spite of his triumphs, was angry with the Navy. It had insisted on conducting the tests, making rules which he said tied his hands, trying its best, he thought, to prevent the success of the demonstration. It had limited the number of planes to be used, specified their types, the weight of bombs to be used for each test; forced the planes to wait in the air after each hit while inspection teams boarded the vessel to examine the damage, thereby exhausting aircraft fuel. It had anchored the ships too far from shore, making the flight of the planes unnecessarily long. Since the ships were anchored and not equipped with anti-aircraft artillery, the Navy Board was afterward able to present the alibi that these were not war conditions.

Had the army air service [he finally wrote in a report to his chief] been permitted to attack as it desired, none of the seacraft attacked would have lasted ten minutes in a serviceable condition. The first provisional air brigade could have put out of action the entire Atlantic fleet in a single attack.

One would think Mitchell would have taken especial pride in the fact that *in spite of all these handicaps* his airmen had done what they had set out to do. But Mitchell's intention had gone further. He wanted to prove that some of the money spent on battleships could be better spent on aircraft. He wanted the nation to build an air force for coastal defense which would keep any invading enemy navy at bay. He wanted also an air force for defense against planes launched from enemy carriers, a threat he already foresaw. He wanted, in short, in 1921 to prevent what happened twenty years later at Pearl Harbor. And, in his report to General Charles Menoher, he repeated his belief in a basic system which would achieve all these things:

> In this connection, an efficient solution of our defensive needs will not exist until a department of national defense is organized with a staff common to all services. Subsecretaries for the Army, the Navy and for the Air Service must be created.

It was the old theme song, sung again and again! Mitchell never left it out of his speeches, his articles, his reports, or his testimony.

In his enthusiasm, however, over ship bombing he exaggerated. He was always talking about proving the battleship to be "obsolete." His supporters kept echoing the word until it rang through the nation. It delighted the money savers. A thousand pursuit planes or five hundred bombers could be built for the price of one battleship. Scrap all the battleships and build a thousand airplanes instead! That was what got the Navy's back up.

Mortally offended, the Navy Board retorted that the battleship was still "the backbone of the fleet." It, too, exaggerated. It made many false statements about the things airplanes could not do. It implied that Mitchell's supporters wanted to wipe out the whole Navy at once and replace it with an air force. At the same time it admitted that a dangerous new weapon had arrived which would create new problems in the construction and protection of ships.

Its answer to Mitchell's accusation that it had rigged the show against him has, as we read it after thirty years, a certain reasonableness. It wasn't trying to prove that aircraft couldn't hit, damage, or even sink a ship. It wanted a scientific test which would show precisely how much damage each weight and kind of bomb could do. It wanted to know how many airplanes could do a job, how far they could fly to do it, how long they could stay in the air, whether direct hits or near misses could do equal damage. What the "mining" or "water-hammer" effect really was. That was why, the board said, it had ordered the inspections after each bombing. Its members were, after all, patriots: they had the good of the country at heart as much as the Army Air Service had—they weren't trying to protect obsolete methods or matériel. The report had its plaintive moments.

Whether all this was true or whether old-time, worn-out traditions were standing in the way of progress can never be proved. Probably there was a combination of both. There were surely some dim-witted admirals, as Admiral Sims and Admiral Fullam (both retired) insisted. It is, of course, easy for a retired admiral to speak the truth in such fashion.

Those who have set Billy Mitchell on a pedestal and will not hear a word against him condemn the old-line services, root and branch. The great achievements of both Army and Navy in two world wars are sufficient disproof of such wholesale abuse. On the other hand, Mitchell made mistakes. He went to extremes to gain his points. Even his "crystal ball," usually so clear, was sometimes clouded. It is, for example, surprising to us today, who know of the later use of radar and proximity fuses to destroy planes from the ground, to read of Mitchell's refusal to see any future in anti-aircraft artillery. It was in his basic theories that Mitchell was usually right rather than in details.

We come in 1922, the year after the bombing tests, into what was perhaps the happiest interval of Billy Mitchell's life. It began at a horse show in Detroit. He had flown out and had his plane ready to fly back. As he walked about the grounds, looking at the horses, he fell into conversation with a slender girl in a riding habit who talked about horses the way he liked to hear them talked about. They walked back to her box together, and he found it was his box, too —one he had been invited to sit in by a Mrs. Miller. The girl turned out to be Mrs. Miller's daughter.

"So, Betty," Mrs. Miller said, "you have met my guest, the General."

"He knows about horses," Betty said.

"Yes," said her mother, "and airplanes——"

What he knew about airplanes Betty discovered later in the afternoon when he took her up. The flight came near ending a romance which had not yet begun. The engine conked when they were more than 2 miles up. Then truly it seemed as if the gods were with Billy Mitchell, for more than half the descent was a glide. After it, she liked the flier better than flight.

He managed to have a good deal of official work in the months after that at Selfridge Field, in Mt. Clemens, close to Detroit where the Millers lived. He took a special interest in the First Pursuit Group commanded by Major Carl

"Tooey" Spaatz, who had been under Mitchell's command in the war and later became a celebrated Air Force general. He would stay at Spaatz's headquarters there, and the major watched the courtship develop with friendly eyes. When Mitchell arrived by plane, a car which he insisted should be capable of an 80-mile-an-hour speed was put at his disposal. It did not take him long to drive from Mt. Clemens to Detroit when the day's work was over. There was no doubt about the work. He made rigid inspections of the group's personnel and equipment and worked constantly to increase its morale and its matériel.

He always flew on these Michigan visits. Once, when he was due for an inspection, his engine went out on the way and he ditched in the Ohio River. It was September and the weather was uncomfortably cold for ditching. Mitchell left the plane and swam ashore. There he took the plane of his aide, who had seen the accident, flew it on to Selfridge Field, and appeared before Major Spaatz still soaking wet and shivering. He would have gone ahead then with the inspection had not the major suggested that he get dry first.

For part of the summer the Millers were in York Harbor, Maine, and Mitchell would fly up there from Washington and stay with them for a day or a week end, landing his plane on the beach. One morning when he was due at breakfast, he did not appear, and Miss Miller wondered at his late sleeping.

Suddenly he came bursting in bringing, it seemed to her, the sea with him.

"I've been up since five," he said. "On the rocks! The

beaches! I've been studying the shells, the starfish, the sea-weed. It's tremendous. The pools left by the tide are full of them."

All through breakfast he talked about the ways of sea fauna and flora, compared the specimens of starfish, shell-fish, and seaweed he had found with those of Hawaii, the Philippines, the Caribbean islands, the French coasts. He was so excited that it seemed as if he had never been in-terested in anything else. As the beginning of a courtship this was singular. It might have bored a hundred of the girls he had known. It did not bore Betty Miller. Behind the fire in his eyes, the flushed excitement of his face, she saw the kind of mind that was her own—eternally in-quiring, learning, interested in every aspect of the beautiful world they lived in.

From the day they were married, Betty Mitchell seems to have had some part in all his activity. She circled the world with him; never drew back from any journey, work, or recreation, however strenuous. She never liked flying but she flew. She became an expert shot; her horsemanship was celebrated. She kept all his complex affairs in order, kept house for him when there was time to have a home, received his hundreds of distinguished visitors, his ene-mies, his companions, and friends of every kind and condi-tion, and charmed them all.

In September, 1923, the month before the wedding was set, Mitchell received orders which fitted his plans per-fectly. They followed, in fact, certain requests he had made. They specified that he should sail from San Fran-cisco on an army transport October 23 for Hawaii "for the purpose of inspecting the Air Service activities in the

Hawaiian Department"; to proceed then to Manila "to inspect Air Service activities in the Philippines"; thence to Japan "to investigate Japanese Air activities" and to China for similar purposes; finally to visit Straits Settlements and India at his own expense on a nonduty status but "for the purpose of familiarizing yourself with the operations of the British Air Base at Singapore and British operations in India."

Now these were extraordinary orders. They not only offered extremely congenial work which Mitchell was anxious to do but they also gave him an extended leave when he would be practically on his own. They came, furthermore, from a War Department he had antagonized, which would be unlikely to go out of its way to meet his wishes. One can only conclude that the men in the upper echelons had decided he was safer out of the country than in it and the further away the better.

Mitchell and his fiancée instantly translated the orders into a honeymoon. The trip would not only meet her love of adventure more than halfway; it would establish at the beginning their intent that she should share his life. And he, of course, would not take time off even for a honeymoon unless he could combine it with work.

In Hawaii he inspected the defenses of the islands. He projected an imaginary war in which Japan would attack and submitted a report on it to General Summerall, the Army Commander at Schofield Barracks. It was not precisely the war which occurred eighteen years afterward, but in some respects it was surprisingly close to it. But in his report, too, there was criticism of the way things were done by both Army and Navy in the Department of Hawaii.

He observed, for instance, as he later told Congress, a dis-
sension between Army and Navy in Hawaii so acute that
the two commanders "would not even go to the same social
functions together"! He reported, too, that each of these
officers had separate plans for what to do in case of war
and that these projects, about which they had not told each
other, were actually in conflict.

Mitchell did not live to see the disastrous results of such
faults, many of which continued until that day of "infamy"
in December, 1941, when a Japanese air attack crippled almost the entire Pacific Fleet as it rested smugly at anchor
in Pearl Harbor.

From Hawaii the Mitchells went to the Philippines. The
general sought out his old antagonist Emilio Aguinaldo,
who received him with friendliness and hospitality. In return Mitchell invited him to make a flight. Aguinaldo had
never been up, but he accepted quietly. He asked that he
be flown over his home town where he had grown up and
where he had many friends. When they were there, the old
man took from his pocket a package of his calling cards and
scattered them over the town.

By stages Mitchell and his bride reached India. The
British viceroy there was an old friend, and he saw to it
that they were welcomed in proper Indian fashion. It was
decided that Mitchell should take a rest from his duties.
He and Betty were, after all, on their honeymoon. For most
of us a restful honeymoon in India implies some luxurious
travel, seeing the Taj Mahal and other great temples, and
spending much time sitting comfortably, gazing long at
exotic views, and eating exotic meals. This was not Billy
Mitchell's idea of rest.

They did see the Taj Mahal. But they also made the unusual journey into the mountains from Darjeeling, going up into Nepal, to the south face of Mt. Everest and near the edge of Tibet. Then, to make the relaxation total, they engaged in a tiger hunt.

Tigers were a menace in Surguja where they had, in that year, forced the inhabitants of thirteen villages to flee their homes. The maharaja was, himself, a champion hunter, and he organized the hunt for the Mitchells on a grand scale with elephants, beaters, and all the rest of the paraphernalia. It was the custom to tie up some animal, such as a water buffalo or other favorite tiger food, and then lie in ambush near the bait until the big striped cat crept up. Shooting it, at this point, was tricky. Unless the shot went true to a vital organ, the wounded beast would turn, and the speed with which it took revenge demanded agility and presence of mind in the hunter.

Big-game hunting, at least in 1923, was not primarily a woman's sport. It did not, however, disturb Betty Mitchell. It fascinated and challenged her. Day after day she watched, waited, shot, and took her chances with the men. Her husband's difficult first shot missed the bull's-eye, and the screaming tiger turned. His second missed entirely; his third was at quarters too close for peace of mind. But his bride's first shot went straight to the heart.

They went to China, Japan, and Korea. They flew over Mukden, in Manchuria. Mitchell experimented with planes used in the Orient's military services wherever he found them. He inspected a fleet of the Japanese navy at Nagasaki and was impressed by its escort of aircraft. "They can fly," he wrote later, "are going to fly, and may end up by developing the greatest air power in the world."

After nine months of "honeymoon" he came back, bringing with him what might be called a blueprint of the future
of the Pacific. In detail it could not be a wholly accurate
forecast, but in its broad strategic lines it could have been
an invaluable guide to the armed forces and, to some extent, to the Department of State. There were files in those
days for such reports—files that were seldom opened—
and into one of them it went. It came out again and was
studied with surprise after almost every place the Mitchells
had explored had passed into Japanese hands. Korea, Manchuria, the ports on the Chinese coast, the Philippines, the
Solomons, the Marianas, the Malay Peninsula, and Java—
all but India had then to be regained piece by piece, and
many thousands died before the outpost flags of the rising
sun came down.

But in the United States in July, 1924, the people had
other things to think about. Along with the climb to paper
prosperity, already begun, the rackets which were a by-
product of national prohibition had securely entrenched
themselves. The madness of the decade had already set
in. A tight-lipped Vermonter who was to maintain a strong
conservatism and a rigid adherence to traditional discipline
stood on the threshold of election to the presidency. He
was dedicated to peace and prosperity to be attained by
caution, shrewdness, thrift, and noninterference with business. Few Americans saw any future but endless green
pastures. There was a general cry for disarmament, for
cutting down the burdens of defense. A year later Messrs.
Kellogg and Briand would solemnly initiate a "pact" to
outlaw war, and representatives of many nations, tongue

in cheek, would solemnly sign it. America would sit down again happily, protected by oceans which to the vision of Billy Mitchell were no wider than irrigation ditches, and engage in its own peculiar pursuits of happiness.

After his journey these things were not heartening to the Assistant Chief of Air Service. But they were nothing to what, while Calvin Coolidge still sat in the White House, was to come.

12

Exile

IN THE HIGH ADVENTURE, the continuing interest, and the mysterious menace of the East, Billy Mitchell could forget the petty jealousies and backbiting of Washington. But when he got back, he found that the Navy had gone on nursing its old grievance, that the Army had sympathized because "the old-timers must stick together," and that there was a solid front against "the air" in both departments. On the other side, welcoming the popular air champion, was a large part of Congress and a public which was constantly growing more aware of the great future of air power.

The Navy's grievance was still the bombing of the ships. First there was the *Ostfriesland* in 1921, which had stunned the admirals; later two other ships had been bombed, the *New Jersey* and the *Virginia*—also by Mitchell's fliers—from the incredible altitude of 10,000 feet and sunk. Immediately after this last demonstration which revived the public cry, "Don't spend our millions on obsolete dreadnoughts!" the naval "experts" worked up a set of alibis, which to us who have seen what happened in World War II are astonishing. They were brought out in a series of articles in the *Army and Navy Journal,* which appeared just as Billy Mitchell was packing for his trip in the fall of 1923.

The *Ostfriesland*, they said, had been sunk by the "mining effect" of bombs dropped near, but not on, the ship. This proved that the *Ostfriesland* was in bad shape. Her upkeep "had been greatly neglected by the Germans after the Armistice. . . . Doubtless all theoretically watertight doors, hatches and air ports were actually not water tight." On the other hand, properly cared-for American ships like the *New Jersey* and the *Virginia* resisted the explosions in the water and were sunk only when bombs landed on their decks. But why did these direct hits sink the American battleships? Because they were old, built before "horizontal armor" was invented. Bombs could not penetrate the decks of a *modern* battleship! Why the *New Jersey* and the *Virginia* were "mere cockleshells as compared with a modern superdreadnought"!

One anonymous editorial explained that the last bombing tests had proved nothing because they were conducted under "artificial conditions." But the real reason for the Navy's rage was that Mitchell's claim that the battleship was obsolete had, as the *Journal* expressed it, "been broadcasted all over the country for many months at the instance of ill-advised air radicals."

There was no doubt in anyone's mind who the "radicals" were. When their leader returned from the Pacific with suitcases full of new alarming reports, the "gold braid" and the "brass" were lined up together against him. In his absence they had allowed the United States Air Services of both Army and Navy be reduced to complete impotence. Now they were ready to reduce him as well.

It was not to be expected that any prophet in 1924 was clairvoyant enough to see that, on a single day seventeen years later, three American battleships would be sunk, one capsized, and four others damaged not to mention severe damage to smaller vessels by a force of 360 carrier-based enemy bombing and torpedo planes. In the Navy such a disaster seemed impossible even on December 6, 1941, the day before it occurred. Yet these ships, it was argued the day after, were "sitting ducks," at anchor, unprepared, in Pearl Harbor on the Hawaiian island of Oahu. It was a carefully planned "sneak attack" in an undeclared war. It was still doubted on December 8 that air power could sink a capital ship under full steam. Yet on the tenth two capital ships which were the pride of the British navy, the dreadnought *Prince of Wales* and the battle cruiser *Repulse*, were sunk by an attack of fifty shore-based Japanese bombers off the Malay Peninsula.

No one could be expected to foresee these precise events in 1924. Yet Mitchell saw the possibility. While others thought in terms of range of a few hundred miles or a 4,000-pound bomb, Mitchell was calculating on the ranges and bombs he knew were coming. Nothing could stop this progress. If the United States did not produce giant bombers and torpedo bombers and a great force of pilots and navigators and gunners and bombardiers and mechanics, someone else would. "I think Japan," he told a congressional committee soon after he got home, "is the second air power [next to Great Britain] in the world or soon will be." Later, when he told another group in Washington that "the island empire of Japan" was owning or aspiring to own all the islands from Kamchatka to the Strait of

Wide World

With Representative P. B. O'Sullivan (left), of Connecticut, at Bolling Field

Brown Brothers

In 1925

Malacca, he was not thinking of harbors or fortresses or naval refueling stations but of air bases scattered through the Pacific from which aircraft could attack.

Although Mitchell may not have had an exact preview of Pearl Harbor—and probably did not have, as he undervalued the aircraft carrier—he understood the vulnerability of unprotected ships both at anchor and under steam, and he most certainly foresaw the sinking of the *Repulse* and the *Prince of Wales* a full twenty years before it happened when he said a speeding ship is an easier target for an airplane than an anchored one.

In Washington in 1924 he jumped quickly into the fight. In a speech in October to the National Aeronautics Association at Dayton, he rubbed salt in the Navy's wound.

He talked again about the bomb tests of 1921 and 1923. He ignored the alibis and the repeated official statements that the battleship was the "backbone" of the Navy. "From a military standpoint," he said, "the future will see seacraft used as auxiliaries for aircraft. The great surface vessels will go." Navy men did not take this as an objective forecast—as one might have said at the start of the automotive era, "The horse will go," or when steamboats first appeared, "The sailing vessel will become obsolete." They took it as deliberate and malicious blasphemy uttered for the specific purpose of angering the old guard.

Actually there was nothing malicious about it. Nothing that Mitchell ever said about air power was malicious. He was not a vindictive person. Personal revenge was not in his character or even, it seems, in his understanding. This is evident again and again from any examination of his behavior, even in his youth. We cannot find an instance of his trying or wanting to "get even" because of some offense. Although he said the most scathing things when he believed them true and necessary to say, he could not understand it when they were taken personally. Although he sometimes unconsciously exaggerated and often seemed, by his emphasis, to exaggerate and although his language was frequently intemperate, these things were the reflection of his anger at conditions of incompetence or neglect rather than at individuals. He did not nurse grievances. He forgot unfair personal attacks. His attitude toward open, declared enemies was astonishingly friendly, as if he had not heard their declarations. He was consistently misjudged in this respect.

Yet these judgments are understandable. His technique in his drive to make the truth understood was peculiarly irritating. His method was constant repetition. He kept using the same words over and over. In his articles we find almost exact, almost verbatim, repetitions of sentences from his testimony before congressional committees or from his public speeches. "A united air force." "The capital ship is obsolete." "Armies will become auxiliary to air power." "Antiaircraft fire is useless." "The Navy can no longer guard our coasts." These things, said again and again, were thrusts that kept old wounds open: they were bound to arouse anger and the accusation of personal malice. As we read today Mitchell's millions of words, this repetition is sometimes tedious, but to him, speaking to many different audiences, it was the way, the only way, to get what he believed to be the truth before the entire country and make it a living, burning issue.

And often enough he was picturesque. To the National Aeronautics Association at Dayton, he said:

In this country today our aeronautical effort is divided between a dozen or more agencies of government, all of which have some function other than aviation. . . . We in the air say: "Give us a chance, give us an opportunity to develop aviation for aviation's sake first and not as an auxiliary to Army and Navy. Let us be a whole dog instead of being the tail of several dogs. . . .

Pursuing the same theme, he talked of fliers as a race apart—as if they were a sort of supermen:

We have today a group of air-going people, and the fraternity among those air-going people that fly in the atmosphere is much greater than has ever been the case with any other group or condition of men.

Although the A-bomb was more than twenty years away, Mitchell spoke as advocates of its offensive use talk today:

You must remember that the air covers the whole country and no part of it is safe from hostile air attack. If we are required to act against an enemy on land we may so smash up his means of production, supply and transportation by bombardment that there is a great probability that armies will never come in contact on a field of battle.

After saying these things to a group of air-minded folk in October, he said them again to the Lampert committee in Congress, and while his friends were shuddering at the probable consequences, he went on to something far worse. He agreed to write a series of three articles for the *Saturday Evening Post*. Now, however much Army and Navy people might deplore a uniformed officer criticizing his service before legislators in Congress or to a group of specialists, it was nothing compared to his appealing to millions of citizens over the heads of his superiors in a popular magazine. To laymen, ordinary, uninstructed men and women, who (although they voted) could never properly evaluate the facts!

When, in December and January, the articles appeared, naval officers were the first to shout, "Insubordination!" This was natural because the articles, as usual, struck hardest at the battleship. Secretary of the Navy Curtis Wilbur told Secretary of War John Weeks that Mitchell had become intolerable. When Weeks postponed action, Wilbur kept at him. Weeks admired Mitchell in many ways. He had been patient before and had intervened to keep Mitchell in office when General Menoher had complained of him. But he finally, as he told Congress, grew "tired of the complaints from the Navy Department" and hauled Mitchell on the carpet for the articles.

Mitchell explained that he had asked permission to write the articles. He produced a letter from President Coolidge in reply. It said:

I do not know of any objection to your preparing some articles on aviation, so far as I am concerned. But, of course, I cannot speak for your superior officers. The matter should be taken up with them and their decision in relation to the articles followed.

Mitchell, said Weeks, had disobeyed the President. He had not "taken the matter up" with his superiors (meaning himself). Oh, yes, he had, Mitchell explained. His commanding officer was General Patrick, Chief of Air Service. Mitchell had taken it up at once with him. Patrick had told him to go ahead. It was not customary, was it, to go over the head of your commanding officer? If anyone was to talk to the Secretary of War, it was Major General Patrick, not his assistant, Brigadier General Mitchell.

Mitchell reported these things to the Lampert committee of Congress which was conducting an exhaustive inquiry into the air services. He offered it as evidence that, in spite of the War Department's published orders to the contrary, officers were being "muzzled."

"The general rule," he said in reply to a question by Congressman Lea, ". . . is that officers shall not give out views . . . without permission of the War Department."

"So," said Mr. Lea, "there is restraint on an officer in advocating a different policy from the announced policy of the department?"

"Yes, sir."

"And restraint," Mr. Lea went on, "upon the presentation of facts upon which Congress might reach a different conclusion . . . ?"

"Yes, sir; that is correct, in spite of published orders allowing freedom of testimony."

Mr. Lea was exasperated.

"How can we ever expect," he said, "to improve inside mistakes or deficiencies in an organization that conceals inside information or prevents those who know it from giving it to a congressional committee?"

"That is exactly the point," Mitchell replied. "It would be impossible to do it."

Finally he made the statement which forced Weeks's hand.

Knowing full well [he told the committee] the possible consequences of any disagreement with the views of the existing agencies of the government . . . I have advised these officers in the services to keep out of the discussions and let me assume all responsibility.

If you talk, he had said in effect to these young flying men, his disciples, you will get into trouble. Your career will be ruined. Your promotion will be deferred. You will be ordered to some remote post. Your family, which is dependent on you, will suffer. You cannot afford the chance. I can. So you had better let me take the rap.

This was the straw that broke Weeks's patience. Harassed by the Navy and embarrassed by the contradictory position Mitchell had placed him in, he did precisely what Mitchell had said the War Department always did to officers who talked. By this act he made a laughingstock of the orders about freedom of speech and sent all the officers who wanted to talk scurrying back to their quarters. Yet it is only fair to remember all the pressures that were upon him. There was a pressure of time, which perhaps was most binding of all. When Mitchell was made brigadier general in 1918, it was a temporary commission. Normally he would have reverted to colonel after the war, but he was appointed for a term Assistant Chief of Air Service in the United States. During that term he could retain the rank of brigadier general. When the term was up, he must be reduced to colonel *unless he was reappointed.*

The term would be up in April, 1925. The President would reappoint him only on the recommendation of the Secretary of War. In February, therefore, we may imagine Secretary Weeks walking the floor at night, wondering if he could conscientiously recommend the continuance in office of this firebrand. Even if he believed with all his heart in Mitchell, it would take a lot of courage to go against the angry opinions of his Army officers and the real fury that raged across the way in the Navy.

Perhaps, if there had been no deadline, he would have postponed writing President Coolidge as he did. The chances are that it would have made little difference in the eventual outcome. Whether or not Mitchell had retained his post, he would certainly have continued his crusade with the same boldness and the same violence.

Because of the publicity given the recent airplane hearings [the Secretary wrote] . . . I think I should explain to you briefly why I am not recommending the reappointment of General Mitchell as Assistant Chief of the Air Service.

The letter went on to say that Mitchell had given a false report of the condition of the Air Service to the congressional committee and that he had given the country the impression that officers of the Army are muzzled and do not dare to express their views.

In addition to these matters, General Mitchell's whole course has been so lawless, so contrary to the building up of an efficient organization, so lacking in reasonable team work, so indicative of a personal desire for publicity at the expense of everyone with whom he is associated that his actions render him unfit for a high administrative position such as he now occupies. I write this with great regret because he is a gallant officer with an excellent war record. . . .

The ax fell. Soon afterward "Colonel" William Mitchell received orders to proceed to San Antonio, Texas, and take up the duties of Air Officer, Eighth Corps, at Fort Sam Houston.

The officers of the Army and Navy sighed with relief. San Antonio was a long way off. To send an officer who had been a "bad boy" to such a place had usually worked. It had taken him out of the limelight. Distance and loneliness had muffled his voice. They were thinking, as they so often did, some fifty years back. In the days of the Indian wars, the pony express, before radio, before the news services and newsreels, and before cheap newsprint, it had been an excellent scheme. Many a "bad boy" had been humbled then by demotion and transfer. But in 1925, where Mitchell went, there, too, went the spotlight. If he was in Texas or on a Pacific island, distance only lent enchantment; whether he was a brigadier general or working on kitchen police, whatever camp contained his quarters, there the reporters would gather with their cameras and notebooks.

Mitchell took his time about going to Fort Sam Houston. He went first to Milwaukee. There he passed an extended leave. He rested after his fashion, enjoyed the company of his wife, danced, went to parties, hunted, finished a book, read, studied and attended horse shows. As reports of these activities and of his debonair acceptance of what to many men would have been mortifying disgrace filtered back to Washington, the "brass" grew uneasy. They were not reassured by the news of his speeches and a publisher's announcement of a "startling" forthcoming book.

As we look back on that time when the spring of 1925 drew into the summer, it seems as if the clouds were already gathering for the storms that would break with violence before the year was over. Two of the storms— one over the Pacific 400 miles east of Hawaii and one over an Ohio town—were not of Mitchell's making. The third, in a Washington winter, was all his.

13

"They Dare Not Tell the Truth"

WHETHER OR NOT the battleship was obsolete in 1925, there was one vessel navigated that year by the United States Navy which was doomed to become so in short order. This ship did not in the least resemble a battleship or a cruiser or a destroyer or any other familiar naval craft. It did not even float on the surface of the water. Being lighter than the air, it floated 1,000 or more feet above the surface and was propelled there by gasoline engines. It was, in short, an airship, more technically a rigid dirigible, of the type that a German family named Zeppelin had developed over many years. The United States Navy had two of these magnificent monsters which, like the dinosaur, were so soon to become extinct: the *Los Angeles*, built in Germany, and the *Shenandoah*, built in Philadelphia.

It is the *Shenandoah* with which we are concerned. It was the *Shenandoah* which Billy Mitchell followed so closely in the news that stormy summer of 1925. She was 680 feet long and looked like an enormous panatela cigar. She was lifted by nineteen gas-filled bags inside her hull.

Her engines, propellers, and crew of forty-three were carried in cars, or gondolas, suspended from it. She was exceedingly impressive and, as aircraft went, costly. The two airships and their accessory equipment had taken fifteen million dollars from the taxpayers, which in 1925 was a good deal of money. No wonder the Navy Department and the President thought that those who had paid for the *Shenandoah* ought to have a good look at her! That is why, in the summer of 1925, the airship was ordered to fly, not with the fleets which plied the ocean, but from city to city in the Midwest, provoking from Billy Mitchell the question, "What business has the Navy over the mountains anyway?"

But the argument was: These people in the inland cities have no way of knowing the Navy exists. They cannot see the ships. And yet they are expected to pay for them just as they pay for the Army, which they can see on maneuvers or in airplanes in the sky. How can these people be expected to encourage their representatives in Congress to vote large appropriations for a navy they have never seen and know little about unless that Navy can devise some means of advertising itself? And what better propaganda could there be than this magnificent monster of the air labeled "U.S. Navy" and known to be navigated by the brave men of that service?

These things were talked about at length as the spring of 1925 drew into the summer. There was an especial need that summer for naval propaganda. For one thing the Navy wanted a larger appropriation than usual when the bills would be introduced in December. Also the Navy wished to share some of the celebrity given the Army for its Round-the-World Flight in 1924 and for the winning by

Army aviators of most of the records for speed, distance, altitude, and endurance. Finally, it smarted under the slaps of Billy Mitchell. Now with the *Shenandoah*, which drew enormous crowds wherever it went, the Navy's prestige could be redeemed. It happened that in September state fairs would be held in many key places of the Midwest. By hovering over these fairs, the *Shenandoah* could draw the crowds and thus boost the fairs, and the crowds in turn could boost the Navy.

It was said that the President had smiled on the venture, which was a rare thing for Mr. Coolidge to do on anything. It was said that he believed the hovering airship would shed glory not only on the Navy but on his Republican administration, elected the previous year. In any case the *Shenandoah*'s skipper, Commander Zachary Lansdowne, was given his instructions, and he did not like them very much.

Lansdowne was an officer in the regular Navy. It was his idea (as it was Mitchell's) that a navy should operate at sea. He had several ideas of working in the *Shenandoah* with the fleet on maneuvers: as an airplane carrier, for instance. He understood storms at sea and believed that the *Shenandoah* could weather them. He was dubious about valley thunderstorms and tornadoes, common in summer. He knew it would be a strain to meet the difficult itinerary covering a number of state fairs considerable distances apart. He was aware that there were inadequate fueling facilities at the designated refueling stops. He wrote of his apprehensions to the Chief of Naval Operations and got a sarcastic reply suggesting that his fears for the airship's safety were fanciful. Lansdowne then asked that the jaunt be postponed for a week to give more time for preparations, and this was refused. The flight was set for September 2. It was to continue until the sixth, covering about 3,000 miles and flying over state fairs at Columbus, Des Moines, Minneapolis, Milwaukee, and Detroit.

The propaganda mission of the *Shenandoah,* imposing as it was, was not the Navy's only venture into the field of public relations that summer. The other was a flight of seaplanes from San Francisco to Honolulu. It was the longest over-water hop yet attempted. According to the magazine *Aviation,* the flight was planned "to offset the impression created by the [Army's] Around the World Flight" of 1924. Three Navy planes were scheduled to take off from San Pablo Bay on August 31: two government-built PN-9s and one Boeing PB-1. Along the 2,000-mile course patrol ships, with which the planes were to be in continuous communication by radio, were posted at intervals of 200 miles.

Both these naval demonstrations were given considerable space in the press so that a large public could follow them in detail.The public learned on the first of September that only the two PN-9s had taken off for Hawaii, the PB-1 having developed engine trouble; on the second it heard that one of the PN-9s had broken down some 300 miles out from the coast and that the other, after flying 1,600 miles of the course alone, was missing. On the fourth it received the final news of the *Shenandoah.* On the sixth it heard from Billy Mitchell.

The log of Commander Lansdowne told the *Shenandoah's* story from the time she cast off from her mooring mast at Lakehurst, New Jersey, at five o'clock in the afternoon of September 2 until twelve hours later, when the writing stopped and the torn skin and bones of the monster were scattered over miles of valley land in Ohio.

She had moved out peacefully enough from Lakehurst. At half past nine that night:

Chambersburg below looks like a picture under a Christmas tree and we think of the kiddies at home and wonder if they are all asleep. Throw kisses to Tom and Billy from the ship in the air. . . .

3:50 A.M. [September 3]. See Cambridge [Ohio] in distance. . . . Storm worst we have encountered to date. . . .

4:55 A.M. Members of crew called from gondola pit and sent into runway to aid in keeping ship on even keel. . . . Hope to ride out storm soon. . . .

Pleasant city seen in distance . . . off course thirty miles south. . . .

Order to throw gasoline tanks given and complied with, but does not aid stability. Radio no better, wind increasing in volume, get chance to——

This sentence was never finished. At an altitude of 3,000 feet the *Shenandoah* was broken by the violence of the storm—a combination of electric storm and "twister"—into three pieces. One of them bearing Lansdowne and thirteen of his crew fell, and all were killed. The forward section with twenty-eight men was floated down to safety 7 miles away.

These accidents, coming so close together, were especially shocking to the public because of the publicity which had preceded them. Turning to the Secretary of the Navy for a statement, the people were even more shocked when Mr. Wilbur pointed to the disasters as proof of the Navy's victory in the Mitchell controversy—that there was no possibility of a hostile air attack!

In view [he said] of . . . the failure of the Hawaiian flight
and the *Shenandoah* disaster we have come to the conclusion
that the Atlantic and the Pacific are still our best defences. We
have nothing to fear from enemy aircraft that is not on this
continent.

In his office in Fort Sam Houston these words struck
Billy Mitchell like a blow between the eyes. Following
news which had already fired his anger, they turned him
white hot. As telegrams poured in on him asking for his
answer to the Navy, he came to a final decision about a
question which, all through the summer, had been shut-
tling back and forth through his mind.

It was a question of loyalties. It was not a new question.
It had been asked since military discipline began in the
world. It is still being asked; there are still two opinions
as to the answer and probably there always will be.

To many officers in the armed forces everywhere—and
especially to graduates of the service academies—loyalty
to the service is paramount. Policies, directives, orders from
above, must not be questioned; obedience and respect for
superiors must be immediate, constant, and automatic. To
cast doubt or suspicion upon any act in the upper echelons
—including the department officials—is insubordination.
What would happen to discipline if everyone were free to
criticize his commanding officer? What sort of example to
junior officers or enlisted men is it for colonels and generals and commanders and admirals to cast slurs upon their
chiefs on staff or board, in ministry or department?

Mitchell's view—and there were many more officers who
agreed with him than dared say so—was that, if there is
a conflict between loyalty to the Army or the Navy and

loyalty to your country, country comes first. In 1925 he sincerely believed that the nation was in danger due to inadequate and wrongly managed national defense. It was not that he foresaw an immediate hostile attack. But he saw the progressive, insidious danger of unpreparedness which, if it continued, would eventually invite attack— as, indeed, precisely it did.

He felt, moreover, that the tradition of silence for officers in uniform was based on wartime necessity, applying with far less rigor in eras of peace. He drew this distinction sharply. In time of war he had not broken the code. But now in 1925, when he saw the people lulled to sleep by the Kellogg-Briand pact to "outlaw war" and all the sweetness and light of Locarno and, at the same time, neglect by the Army and the Navy of the one strategy which he knew would dominate the next, inevitable war, he could not reconcile his conscience to a silence he regarded as treason.

There are those who say that, feeling as he did, he should have resigned from the Army first and talked afterward. But Mitchell's belief was that there was a better chance of effecting the reforms by staying in. If he talked in uniform, he knew that he would be disciplined, probably by a court-martial, but the very discipline itself would point up the seriousness of the conditions. That an officer was willing to risk the ruin of his career in order to speak the truth was evidence that the situation was desperate indeed!

There are also those who feel that Mitchell went to unwarranted extremes in his accusations. It is probable, however, that in the first flush of his anger anything less would have been impossible for him. We have seen how closely this impulse to violent, explosive expression of righteous indignation was identified with his character.

Whatever may be the rights and wrongs of all these arguments—and they are likely to go on forever—the fact was that Billy Mitchell acted the instant his decision was made. For two days, day and night, he paced the floor of his office in the hot Texas garrison, dictating to his stenographer. On the fifth of September he gave to three San Antonio papers and to the Associated Press copies of a statement, seventeen typewritten pages long, which was called "the most daring indictment of the War and Navy Departments ever made by an officer."

I have been asked [it began] from all parts of the country to give my opinion about the reasons for the frightful aeronautical accidents and loss of life, equipment and treasure that has occurred during the last few days. This statement therefore is given out publicly by me after mature deliberation and after a sufficient time has elapsed since the terrible accident to our naval aircraft, to find out something about what happened.

About what happened, my opinion is as follows: These accidents are the direct result of the incompetency, criminal negligence and almost treasonable administration of the national defense by the Navy and War departments.

It was this crescendo which, in the second week in September, echoed round the world. The flaming words "incompetency," "criminal negligence," and "treasonable administration" were picked up everywhere and put into headlines. Millions of people who read them read nothing else in the statement. They were hailed as courageous and condemned as intemperate by editors of every kind and condition of newspaper and periodical. They split the people, official and unofficial, in Washington and out of it, into two groups. If Mitchell's words were intemperate, they were nothing compared to those that were used about him. One congressman in a single sentence compared him with Alexander, Napoleon, Caesar, Robert E. Lee, Foch, and Pershing, and one admiral referred to him as a vulture posing as an eagle, adding, however, that he was probably of unsound mind. The commonly temperate *New York Times* in an editorial entitled "Both Insubordination and Folly" said, "This is not language becoming an officer and a gentleman."

But the statement went on for some 8,000 words after this preamble. It became exceedingly specific. It asserted:

All aviation policies, schemes and systems are dictated by the non-flying officers of the Army and Navy who know practically nothing about it. The lives of the airmen are being used merely as pawns in their hands. . . . The airmen themselves are blinded and bulldozed so that they dare not tell the truth. . . . The conduct of affairs by these two [War and Navy] departments, as far as aviation is concerned, has been so disgusting in the last few years as to make any self-respecting person ashamed of the clothes he wears. Were it not for the patriotism of our air officers and their absolute confidence in the institutions of the United States, knowing that sooner or later existing conditions would be changed, I doubt if one of them would remain with the colors. . . .

The unhappy men on the Hawaiian trip, the statement said, were given planes of an old design, untried for such a flight, with no provision for refuelling in the air, with the patrol ships too few and improperly placed. He referred to the leading PN-9 carrying the flight commander, John Rodgers, as a "really good-for-nothing, big lumbering flying boat." He said the *Shenandoah* was 50 per cent overweight in her structure; that the Navy had economized on her expensive helium gas; that her frame had been strained by an earlier storm; that she was on an improper mission—being over land instead of water—for propaganda purposes; that the Weather Bureau, of the Department of Agriculture, "primarily organized to turn out weather reports affecting onions, cabbage and other crops," could hardly be expected to forecast for aircraft; and that the accident was due to "incompetence in the Navy Department and the criminal negligence in the ordering of this trip."

The statement went on to a scathing indictment of the Navy's Arctic expedition with "the little jitneys they took up there" and turned finally to the War Department, which had given false information to the public about the effectiveness of anti-aircraft fire, had endangered the lives of fliers by forcing them to use "flaming coffins," yet continued to hold down their pay, and had done "nothing . . . to develop air power." It concluded:

As a patriotic American citizen, I can stand by no longer and see these disgusting performances by the Navy and War Departments, at the expense of the lives of our people and the delusion of the American public.

The bodies of my former companions in the air moulder under the soil in America, and Asia, Europe and Africa—many, yes, a great many, sent there directly by official stupidity. . . . We would not be keeping our trust with our departed comrades were we longer to conceal these facts.

This, then, is what I have to say on this subject and I hope that every American will hear it.

Looking back over the country's newspapers of the period, it seems as if every American must have heard part of this attack at least. A few days later, however, Mitchell came out with a second statement, which was far more constructive and which doubtless had far fewer readers. In it he outlined what should be done. He repeated his belief that the nation should have a secretary of air to take charge of civil as well as military aeronautics, encourage commercial air transport, and lay down airways for it. Under this secretary there should also operate the military air force, but over him would be a secretary of national defense who would also control Army and Navy. The statement went into detail on these matters and cited the adoption of the system by other nations.

A final paragraph explained that the first attack was meant to be impersonal:

The terrible condition in our national aeronautics today is not so much the result of the absolute ignorance of individuals because often these are selected on the principle of saying "tag, you're it: go play with aviation," when they know nothing about it and are really more to be pitied than blamed. The trouble is with the system, and we flying people insist that our views be known and weighed by the American public.

On the thirteenth of September, Mitchell was answered by Rear Admiral William A. Moffett, Chief of the Bureau of Naval Aeronautics, who, though he mentioned no names, left little doubt as to whom he meant.

Destructive criticism [the admiral said] has shaken the confidence of the country in its government. Examples of disloyal conduct have sown the seeds of discord in aviation establishments. False charges have branded loyal servants of the people with the stigma that denial can hardly efface. The revolutionary methods of the Communists have been invoked to overcome the opposition of loyal men who have sought to thwart the ambition of unscrupulous self-seekers. . . .

It is interesting to observe that even in 1925 persons accused of opprobrious conduct were compared with communists. Admiral Moffett went on to say that appeals by military officers "over the heads of the Congress to the people . . . might be the opening wedge for military dictatorship in the United States."

This was something of an about-face on the part of Admiral Moffett, who until then had usually been on Mitchell's side. He had upheld Mitchell's contentions on battleship bombing. He had deplored the low appropriations for aeronautical development. He had, himself, climbed so far out on a limb in the interests of aviation that there had been talk of a reprimand. But somehow Mitchell's violence had got under his skin and moved him to even greater intemperance than Mitchell's in his reaction. Some of Billy Mitchell's friends were sorry he had antagonized this champion of so many of his earlier attitudes.

The fact that both Navy and Army people called Mitchell's statement nonsense did not prevent the President from wondering how much truth there might be in it. Too big a public was demanding answers to the questions Mitchell had brought up. The only way to appease these people was by an investigation. Actually Congress had already conducted an exhaustive investigation of the Air Services, but that had been before the accidents and before Mitchell's attack. It had backed Mitchell's earlier arguments. Perhaps now another "nonpolitical" group would oppose him. It was said that the President hoped so. It would be logical for him to want a whitewash of the secretaries he had appointed. Yet, as we look back at the inquiry made by this President's Aircraft Board, it seems to have been perfectly honest, if unintelligent, and composed of fair-minded men.

In any case Mitchell was immediately asked to give all the testimony he wished. On September 22 he was relieved of duty at Fort Sam Houston, and shortly after, he was ordered to report before the board on Monday, September 28, at 10:30 A.M.

He arrived in Washington with his wife the Friday before at dusk. Several posts of the American Legion were at Union Station to meet him. Legionnaires bore him out of the station on their shoulders, cheering. Outside he was cheered again, and the crowd became so "rambunctious" that the police had to interfere. Then the major who, less than twenty years later, was to become famous as General "Hap" Arnold drove the Mitchells away in his car. On Saturday the "Forty and Eight" of the Legion escorted him in a parade down Pennsylvania Avenue, and finally his enthusiastic Washington friends gave a barbecue in his honor. Then Billy and Betty Mitchell fled to the home they had bought at Middleburg, Virginia, near the head of the Shenandoah Valley, and spent Sunday there going over the 800 pounds of papers Billy had brought with him to support his case.

Meanwhile, the missing PN-9 seaplane had been picked up and towed to port by a submarine. Its gas had given out, and it had simply flopped on the water. The crew had rigged a sail on it, and for nine days it had moved, lonely, through the Pacific. Commander Rodgers and his crew, though nearly exhausted and starved, survived. Rodgers then showed his loyalty to the Navy by denying Mitchell's accusations of negligence.

The most important event of the summer in Mitchell's

personal life was the birth, in August, of a daughter. Immediately after his arrival in Washington there appeared on the front page of a Washington newspaper a photograph of the colonel with the month-old Lucy in his arms. It is, perhaps, his most charming portrait. Thoroughly disarming to critics of his "arrogance," it shows him in one of his tenderest moods when all his pride and pleasure seem focused on the baby. It is hardly surprising that public and press, politicians, bureaucrats, and soldiers were baffled by the contradictory appearances of this astonishing figure. He is a firebrand, a stormy petrel, an eagle, and a vulture; vain, contemptuous, courageous, a martyr to the truth— and suddenly everything is dissolved in a father's affection for a tiny girl!

14

"Guilty As Charged"

THE PRESENCE OF Billy Mitchell in Washington after his six months' absence was electric. It promised the kind of thrill the capital especially enjoys in an otherwise unexciting interval of peace. But it also promised the kind of debate between government and people which keeps a democracy's heart beating and its blood circulating.

Mitchell was never more bristling with energy or less downhearted. Dressed in a gray tweed suit, a soft shirt, and a gray sombrero with a bright hatband, carrying always his light cane, smiling his hearty welcome to friend and foe alike—waving his large gloved hand across a street, unconscious of the cameramen jostling each other for a shot—he showed no awareness of shadow to come. When a foreboding friend hinted at the court-martial, he acted as if it was the friend, not he, who needed cheering up. He kept up the spirits of his wife in the dreariest hours, diverted and amused her. His challenge was: "Suppose they do find me guilty? Guilty of what? I have committed no crime! Suppose I am dismissed? Well . . . I've always wanted to hunt big game in Africa. Disgrace? What is the disgrace?"

These were the things that made the people who hated

Billy Mitchell hate him more. If he had been contrite, despondent with regret for anything he had done, there might have been some appeasement of the bitterness against him. But it was his assurance of rightness, the armor against criticism that was as much a part of him as his skin, that drove his enemies wild. They would rather he answered an accusation with a fist than with a smile. His reply to someone who called him names because of his views was simply, "No, wait a minute, old man. Let me tell you why you are wrong."

He was so concentrated on the facts, the subject, the argument, that he would often ignore personal attack. This unconscious self-confidence, this unquestioning sureness that he was right, this apparent insensitiveness, made people cry out in their rage, "Get rid of him; crucify him!"

Yet they never did "crucify" Billy Mitchell. The myth of his "crucifixion" is a creation of sentimentalists. The mawkish nonsense of his "crown of thorns"—an image kept alive through session after session of Congress for twenty years —was sometimes useful but never true. Neither government nor Army nor fickle press ever seriously hurt him, and his words went marching on—slowly perhaps but without interruption.

When he appeared before the President's Aircraft Board, his scorn was as high as ever; his sharp words had lost none of their edge.

In the Army [he said] we have no air force, none whatever, either in matériel—that means airplanes and equipment—in personnel (pilots, observers, gunners, or mechanics)—or in operations—that is, method of using it. The effigy of this thing that is held up before the American people consists of about 12,

now old and worn, pursuit airplanes . . . 22 bombers, designed
seven years ago and worn out by constant service and of ob-
solescent type. All other aviation consists of the DH-4 airplanes
with the Liberty engine, designed during the war, which are
neither fish, flesh, nor fowl as they are neither attack, bombardment, pursuit or observation planes. They are worn out; they
are dangerous; they are incapable of performing any functions
of a modern air force. Our pilots, the best in the world, really
amount to not over 450, of all categories. The reserves are a
myth. They have no service matériel to fly in and no manner
of keeping up to modern conditions. They are growing old. We
have no corps of observers . . . no rated machine gunners.
Our so-called mechanics are recruited according to the Army
system. . . .

He went on to warn of disaster if war came; of the
years it would take to organize our defense in the air
against a "first class power, either of Europe or of Asia"—
already equipped, as such powers were, with great independent armies of the sky. He talked of the difficulty of
catching up in production of aircraft and the training of
men in this utterly new and difficult field of war.

And so, for some 50,000 words, answering questions,
countering the attacks of generals and admirals, Billy
Mitchell went on erecting his own gallows and, at the
same time, building a solid structure for the future of the
national defense. For there it was in the end, the old, only
answer, the dream that had to come true: an air force on
its own, not under the command of men who thought in
terms of limited ground objectives, but following the curves
of the earth to strike, before all armies and navies, at the
heartland of an enemy.

Yet with all Mitchell's eloquence and that of his growing

body of disciples among the airmen, the President's board refused to believe. It found the conservative old generals and admirals more convincing. When these solid, solemn men, whose vision was still back before World War I, spoke of airplanes as scouts and patrols, the solid, solemn members of the board nodded their heads. Yes, yes, aviation had proved its value in observing the movements of the enemy army and in directing the fire of our own artillery. Yes, yes, airplanes were even better than balloons for this purpose. And, on the ocean, airplanes were the "eyes of the fleet." It had been proved that they could find hostile ships and report back so that our own ships could go in pursuit and destroy the enemy by gunfire. Yes, indeed, airplanes were valuable adjuncts to the Army and the Navy and, therefore, must be kept under Army and Navy command.

But when Mitchell and the fliers said that aircraft had become a striking force able to smash factories and railroads with bombs and that they could defend a coast by sinking invading ships, the members of the board shook their heads. No, no, they said, reports of bombardment in the war (now seven years before) had been greatly exaggerated; no indeed, there had been no marked progress since; there was still considerable question about sinking the ships. These were callow youths talking, "prima donnas" someone called them, undisciplined, insubordinate—as Mitchell had proved—not to be taken seriously. The board closed its hearings and in due time reported:

We do not consider that air power, as an arm of the national defense, has yet demonstrated its value. . . . We believe that such independent missions as it is capable of can be better carried out under the high command of the Army or Navy as the case may be.

If the pilots and crews of bombers in World War II or the men who have flown in "MIG Alley" have read these words of 1925, they must have found them curious—hardly credible.

By the time the President's Aircraft Board closed its hearings, Billy Mitchell had received copies of the War Department's charges against him. He was given some three weeks to prepare his defense before the court-martial would open. From the group of lawyers who were eager to act for him, he chose Frank Reid, a congressman from Illinois, who had been on the Lampert committee of the House and who was almost as expert in the theory of military aviation as Mitchell himself. It proved to be a brilliant choice. It was Reid who gave the trial its character, its direction, and much of its importance.

Many of those who have written about Mitchell have treated the court-martial as if it had been the most significant event of his life. Some biographers have even regarded it as the climax and the end—like the hanging of John Brown—as if after it only the soul of Billy Mitchell went marching on. It provided, of course, a good take-off for a legend, and the Mitchell myth, which is still good for a sob or so from several Senators and Representatives, was built upon it.

From this distance—more than a quarter century away —it is easier to separate the legend from the fact. In the sweep of Mitchell's life across a world which changed as the world never changed before, the court-martial seems only an incident, one of those things which had to happen because it was written in the book. Let us look for an instant at what was (and still is) written in the book and on which the Army in cases like this has to act. It is called the ninety-sixth article of war. Here it is:

> Though not mentioned in these articles, all disorders and neglects to the prejudice of good order and military discipline, all conduct of a nature to bring discredit upon the military service . . . shall be taken cognizance of by a . . . court-martial and punished at the discretion of such court.

It says nothing about the motive for bringing discredit. It says nothing about loyalty to the service coming in conflict with loyalty to country. It does not allow for the "conduct" which brings discredit on the service being a statement of truth. True or false, once it brings discredit, the goose of the accused is cooked. Under military law the court-martial which tried Billy Mitchell had no alternative but to find him guilty. His conduct was "of a nature" to bring discredit: that was all there was to it. As *The New York Times* had said editorially back in September:

> If the War Department decides to call Colonel Mitchell before a court-martial, the simple issue will be whether he has been guilty of disrespect to his superiors and insubordination. It will not be mismanagement of the air service.

And yet, to the astonishment of most observers, once the trial got under way, the court decided to throw open the doors to all the evidence the defense cared to introduce. Whether these generals who composed the court really wanted to be fair, whether there was doubt among them as to Mitchell's motive or the truth of his fiery words, whether they were honestly anxious to learn more about military aviation even after all the inquiries and investigations and boards and committees, or whether (knowing what the end must be) they wanted to escape criticism for steam-rolling the trial, they let Mitchell, his counsel, and their witnesses talk. They let them talk about the *Shenandoah* and the "flaming coffins," the bombing of ships, the negligence of the Navy, and the desirability of a separate air force, and Frank Reid paraded such a galaxy of witnesses to these truths that the trial became a milestone in the march of the air-power crusade.

The words that were said need no repetition here: they were the same words that had been said again and again before—in Congress and out—printed in the papers, in the magazines, in volumes of records. To give a day-by-day narrative of what went on for seven weeks in that queer, little, shabby Washington courtroom would be tedious and a mere repeating of every chapter of Mitchell's life since the war. Yet we cannot doubt that it was good for the future of American aviation that they *were* repeated there where the spotlight was so bright. After that trial any American who did not know the score on Air versus Army and Navy had no excuse.

But there were some high and humorous points and some splashes of color that must be remembered in any Mitchell story. One was the background against which the scenes were acted. No one has ever discovered why the War Department picked its oldest, most bedraggled building for this court-martial. Was it to humiliate the accused? If so, it only succeeded in mortifying and giving discomfort to some of the most distinguished generals of the Army. The building was one which had been abandoned even as a warehouse. Even the rats had left it. The room picked for the court was on the second floor. Only a handful of the thousands of spectators who came to watch got up there, and those who did, found it hard to get out again. This resulted in some diverting low comedy on the first day of the trial.

It is customary in a court-martial for the court to deliberate privately on each charge as it is read to determine jurisdiction. Normally spectators are ordered to leave during these conferences. In this room such "clearing of the court" was impossible. It was decided, therefore, to have the members of the court retire instead to an anteroom for each session. As there were eight charges, the nine generals and one colonel composing the court were obliged to rise and file solemnly out of the room eight successive times. This became so much like a dance in a musical comedy that the crowd finally broke into frank roars of laughter— a demonstration to which West Pointers are not accustomed.

But if the courtroom was colorless, the beribboned court was anything but. The four major generals and five brigadiers and one colonel who, after three members had been challenged and excused, composed the court were celebrated for their achievements in the war and revered for special talents. They included Robert Howze, Commander of the Fourth Division, AEF, William Graves who had helped 2,000 Czech refugees escape from Bolshevik Russia, Edward King who had been aide to two presidents, and Douglas MacArthur, son of a famous general and on the way toward even greater fame himself. Billy Mitchell knew most of them, and even as they stood arrayed against him, he still thought of them as his friends.

But Mitchell, in his appearance, presented a sharp contrast to these stern characters. As we look today at the photographs of the trial, the generals seem to represent the past and Mitchell the future. They wore the stiff "strait jackets" which in 1925 were still the Army uniform. Mitchell wore the easy roll collar that, as a special concession, had been awarded aviators. The generals had the ramrod bearing of old soldiers; Mitchell the ease, suppleness, and grace of today's pilots. The generals were solemn in the performance of their duty; Mitchell met his "disgrace" with smiles and waved greetings to his friends. Next to him, day after day, sat his lovely wife, whose spontaneous gestures of affection and encouragement delighted everyone who saw them. With him, during much of the trial, was his staunch sister Harriet.

A high point in the trial came when the defense introduced Admiral Sims. This grand, old, bearded officer, who in 1925 stood higher in reputation than anyone in the Navy, had the look of a conservative. Yet when he spoke, he shattered every reactionary naval tradition. He said the battleship was no longer a capital ship, that the carrier had replaced it. He said that any invading fleet could be destroyed by a properly organized land-based air force. He assailed the motives of the Navy Department in ordering the *Shenandoah* to fly over state fairs. He stated that most admirals were hidebound; that all who had not attended the Naval War College were uneducated. When the prosecutor read the names of seven such admirals and asked if the witness considered them "hidebound, unfitted, and uneducated," he replied in a voice that almost shook the building, "I certainly do!"

Sims was, to be sure, retired and so beyond the reach of punishment for his words, but he cheered many a junior officer in his service whose lips were sealed.

As the weeks dragged on, it was inevitable that the Mitchells should feel the strain. Yet behind the scenes they made the best of it. They lived in an apartment in the Anchorage Hotel which had been given them by friends. Under the terms of his technical arrest Mitchell was not allowed to leave the Washington district. Yet even with this confinement and the stresses of his endless conferences with counsel, he never forgot to divert and cheer his wife. She remembers an incident that was characteristic.

It was her birthday. He had never forgotten her birthday. This time, under the nervous tension, she thought he had. All day he had been away. He came in hurriedly at dinnertime.

"Come on," he said, "let's go to the Amalfi," mentioning an Italian restaurant, but still saying nothing of her birthday. She was certain he had not remembered. She said she would change her dress and go.

"No, no, Betty," he said. "Don't wait. I'm hungry. Come along."

And he almost pushed her into the little automatic elevator.

To her surprise the elevator stopped at the second floor instead of going on to the lobby. When the door opened, she saw bright lights and heard many voices in a gay room.

"Let's stay here a minute," Billy said, and suddenly she was in the midst of a large birthday party which he had arranged weeks before. All their friends were there; a table groaned with food; waiters moved about with champagne.

At the court-martial trial

With his wife and Lucy in Washington

The end came on December 17. On that morning it was the turn of his counsel to sum up. But Mitchell knew that it was useless. He had seen the handwriting on the wall. He said to the court:

My trial before this court-martial is the culmination of the efforts of the General Staff of the Army and the General Board of the Navy to deprecate the value of air power and keep it in an auxiliary position, which absolutely compromises our whole system of national defense.

These efforts . . . were begun as soon as the sound of the cannon had ceased on the Western front in 1919. When we sunk the battleships off the Virginia Capes in 1921, and again in 1923, and proved to the world that air power had revolutionized all schemes of national defense, these efforts were redoubled and have continued to this day.

The truth of every statement which I have made has been proved by good and sufficient evidence before this court, not by men who gained their knowledge of aviation by staying on the ground and having their statements prepared by numerous staffs to bolster up their predetermined ideas, but by actual fliers who have gained their knowledge firsthand in war and in peace. . . .

To proceed with the case would serve no useful purpose. I have therefore directed my counsel to entirely close our part of the proceeding without argument.

At that point the prosecutor, or Assistant Trial Judge Advocate, delivered a speech which must have surprised those who had called Mitchell's language "intemperate." Mitchell, he said, was "flamboyant, self-advertising, wildly imaginative, destructive . . . and never overly careful as to the ethics of his methods." He called Admiral Sims "egomaniacal" and "narrow-minded." The outburst, however, was quite superfluous. The chapter was already closed. The court's vote, by secret written ballot, was perfunctory. It found the accused guilty and sentenced him "to be suspended from rank, command and duty, with forfeiture of all pay and allowances for five years." "The court," the announcement added, "is thus lenient because of the military record of the accused during the World War."

The verdict and the sentence surprised many people because it did, indeed, seem lenient. Why had the court not dismissed him summarily and completely from the Army? In Italy the great airman Douhet, who had spoken out much as Mitchell had spoken, had been imprisoned for his conduct! Presently, however, there appeared to Mitchell's supporters to be a trick in the verdict. It suspended his rank and pay, relieved him from all duty. *But it kept him in the Army.* It kept him from other occupations. And it also kept him from talking.

To Billy Mitchell this would have been intolerable. His conscience would not permit his silence. On January 27, 1926, therefore, he resigned from the Army. This may not have been easy to do. For all its failings the Army gets a hold on its officers and men which is hard to break. In Cuba, in the Philippines, in Alaska, in Europe, and in the Far East, it had given adventure, excitement, fun, friendships, and rare opportunities for patriotic service to Billy Mitchell.

Whatever his feelings, however, he showed no regret. The stories that were told of his midnight sorrow, his trembling hand on the signature, his bowed head, and his bitterness are legend, not fact.

President Coolidge accepted the resignation, and on February 1 it took effect.

15

Vision of a New World

SOME FORTY MILES west of Washington in the Piedmont Valley of Virginia lies the village of Middleburg. It is in the heart of hills known as the Bull Run Mountains; to the west is the Blue Ridge. In the country round it, horses are still more important than politics or business. The owners of the land, which is punctuated by the towns of Middleburg, Upperville, Aldie, Leesburg, and Boyce, breed horses, school them, show them, race them, and ride them to hounds. It is gentle country in an easy climate; life is leisurely there, and it seems a long way from the turmoil of the capital. It is the sort of place a busy and harassed man might keep in the back of his mind as a retreat—a week-end or vacation escape, a kind of dream place—for nothing mean or tormenting could very well follow you to Middleburg: it would dissolve there in the lazy sunshine, or the dogs would bark it away.

That was how Billy Mitchell thought of Middleburg. His wife thought of it more permanently, perhaps, as a home. The Mitchell estate, Boxwood, was away from the town in rolling country with fine hill and valley views, a lot of cleared land fenced for the horses, wood lots good

169

for shooting, and streams for trout in the seasons. The stable held more than twenty horses and was usually full of fine, blooded animals with distinguished pedigrees; some belonged to the Mitchells and some had been sent to them for training. When a show was in the offing, three or four of the best animals were prepared for the ring, from which they usually walked away with a blue or red rosette.

Here the Mitchells had gone when they could in the days before the trial, and once during it they had been allowed to spend a week end here. When the trial was over and the colonel (who after that was never called anything but General) had left the Army for good, Boxwood would have been the logical place for him to settle down. It offered all his favorite recreations. His 200 guns, countless fly rods, trophies won in every sort of adventure from war to sport, the tiger skins from India, and his well-digested books were all assembled there. And he had earned a rest. Few soldiers had fought harder or spoken more cogently for their country. Very few had risked their lives as often. He was forty-six years old, an age when men are supposed to take it easy. But Billy Mitchell rarely did what he was supposed to do. There was no "settling down" desire in him: from his earliest childhood he had been geared to action.

What is in him [Clinton Gilbert wrote] is innate, a love of speed, of excitement, a capacity to throw himself utterly into whatever he does, reckless physical daring, self-confidence, a politician's love of applause, . . . delight in his fellow men aristocratic contempt for dull, commonplace and ponderous caution. What isn't in him is poise, balance, sober regard for consequences, capacity to wait upon time's slow justification.

And it wasn't in him to retire. The reporters who wrote stories about his withdrawing to Virginia to be a gentleman-farmer and stock breeder were simply accepting the legend of his defeat by the Army. That would have put him in the rear guard—intolerable for the leader he had always been.

He has always been cheating time [Clinton Gilbert wrote]. He is on more intimate terms with the future than any wise man, especially any army bureaucrat has a right to be. Naturally he was one of the first army flyers. . . . Before there were airplanes there was automobiles. And he always drove the highest powered, speediest car possible in the wildest way possible. And before there were automobiles there were horses. And he always rode horses as if he were the original Centaur. . . .

At the army posts it was always he who got up the dances, led the cotillions, was chairman of the committee of entertainments. He has gone through life with his fingers on the "joy stick," long before "joy sticks" were invented. And when he dances . . . he is rhythm itself, so thoroughly does he abandon himself to the music. And when he goes into a controversy he goes into it as he does into a dance, throwing the whole of himself into it, which is one reason why in the end the controversy "gets" him.

No, there was no place for Mitchell in the rear, and Boxwood in 1926 presented no rest in the sylvan shade. And yet in the next ten years it became more and more of a headquarters. It was something to which he always came back. In this way it was novel in his life. Before, in his incessant movement over the country and over the world, there had been no haven to which he could return—indeed, no home. Though he continued to stray away on all sorts of ventures, Boxwood with his wife and daughter and, later, a son in it became a kind of magnetic center, and gradually he was spending more and more time there.

They went there when the trial was over. But when he resigned from the Army, Billy Mitchell tossed his uniform to his wife to put away in camphor and started across the country. It was still early in February. He had no intention of letting the public cool off. To him the issue of the air was hotter than ever: the trial and conviction had put it red and glowing on the anvil, and now was the time to strike. And now he could talk, how he could talk!

He called it a "barnstorming tour." He went from town to town in the West, taking the story to the people. What he really achieved on this trip was proof that the Army had not beaten him. There he was, the same old Billy Mitchell, dynamic, fiery, compelling. The uniform had nothing to do with it. This was important. Whether his talks were more convincing than they had been or his propaganda wider in its appeal, the fact of his barnstorming kept his disciples with him. There are reasons to believe that, as a lecture tour, it was not wholly a success. Perhaps in that time of peace and growing prosperity people were not anxious to hear about threats of war or needs for defense. But to the young Army and Navy fliers it meant much. Mitchell's conviction had been a blow between the eyes for the men who knew the real score about military flying. If, for the briefest time, then, he had quit or shown any sign of being stunned or disheartened, a weakening of morale might have spread like disease among these men who could not speak.

Yet in those two months of Mitchell's constant motion,

Boxwood played a part that was new in his life. In Boxwood there was a sort of control tower or message center. To it he wrote every day—news of his talks and audiences and welcoming dinners and of his detours pursuing the ducks and prairie chickens in South Dakota, the bass in Rainy Lake in Minnesota, tarpon in the Gulf of Texas, trout and big game along the border between Colorado and New Mexico. But into Boxwood also poured the great volume of his "fan mail." Mrs. Mitchell answered all of it. There were many letters from boys in high schools in the towns where Mitchell had talked. "Dear General," they wrote, "We are planning a debate. Resolved: That the United States should have a separate department of air service. . . ." They wanted material right from the horse's mouth for their arguments. Mrs. Mitchell took special care with these. She sent mimeographed material, clippings, everything that would help. She knew how seriously her husband took the young people from whom the fliers of the future would come.

She was so busy with these things that it was surprising she was able to do so much else at Boxwood to make the kind of home the "general" would want more and more to live in. But in this important early spring season she oversaw the planting of the crops. She rode and jumped and schooled and prepared for the coming shows the brown five-year-old Bull Run, the bay Boxwood—sixteen-three— the thoroughbred Eclipse, and the three-year-old sorrel gelding Flood Tide. And she took care of Lucy.

When he came home at the end of March, Mitchell found Boxwood a good place for work as well as play, and in the years that followed, it became increasingly important to him. The house was spacious, built of the native field stone more than a hundred years back—built for the old southern abundance and hospitality. Some of the rooms were big enough for a large ball. With the great rooms opening into one another with wide doorways, with a fireplace in every room, it was a perfect party house. We may imagine it on Christmas or New Year's, flooded with firelight and candle-light, with a gay crowd of men and girls and women and boys from all the countryside dancing half the night.

And there were many special things that endeared Box-wood house to those who lived there. In one of the hearths there was a stone with the print of a dinosaur's foot in it—facing out as if it had walked out of the fireplace, which was almost big enough. There was a friendly ghost at Boxwood which everyone heard but only the dogs saw. Mitchell's study was at the end of a long wing. The hall leading to it was hung with the heads of animals. In the study were the special books on wars, flying, ancient history, birds, trees, wild animals, horses, firearms, fish, and science that Billy Mitchell knew by heart and the photographs of friends and planes—mementos of old adventures. Outside the west window his wife planted his favorite tree, a larch, on one of his birthdays.

At an age when most small girls are swinging or play-ing in the sand, Lucy was on the back of one of the big hunters. About this time Billy, Jr., came along. To the children their father was a continuing source of delight. He amused and thrilled them with stories of his adventures. There could, of course, have been a different dozen every night and the reservoir would not be emptied. He taught them to find their way over the great globe in his study, to feel the roundness of the earth, the directness of flight over it, and the importance in the future of every remotest spot on it. To them, in their lifetime, nothing would be inaccessible, space would dissolve, time would acquire new meanings.

The children have never understood the talk about Mitchell's arrogance or conceit. All they remember is gentleness and patience or a companionableness, indoors and out, in good times and bad. Lucy tells the story, for instance, about her glasses. She developed trouble with her eyes, and spectacles were prescribed. But she wouldn't wear glasses. She wouldn't and she wouldn't. An impasse developed. Mitchell against Mitchell, a truly formidable situation. One night the general came home with a pocketful of glasses of every size. He fitted a pair to every member of the family, to each of the guests (of which Boxwood was always full), to the maids and the cook, and to himself. Next morning at breakfast only one member of the household had bare eyes. The protests were forgotten, and there were tears of jealousy until the general produced Lucy's prescribed glasses.

Boxwood became a headquarters, but it was too small to hold him all the time. He spent many months on the coast building a cabin cruiser—largely with his own hands. He called her the *Canvas Back* and sailed her from Hampton Roads to the Bay of Fundy. In all the harbors the little boat was known and welcomed, and wherever there was a ship of the Navy, it blew its whistle in salute—a defiant salute, sure enough, that said, "We see you, Billy; we know you're still there. We're still against you, but we can't help saluting a fighter!"

He kept up his correspondence and wrote his friends on every subject. In a letter to John Cudahy, before going into a scathing attack on President Hoover, he wrote:

I have twenty-two horses in the stable now ready for hunting. . . . I have made all these horses jump my big plank fences and they are perfectly quiet in the field but to . . . hunt these things hard before their splint bones solidify in their legs and their sasamoids, tendons and joints become solidified, would mean just entirely ruining them.

In 1931, when Japan defied the League of Nations in Manchuria, he wrote to Arthur Brisbane:

The Japanese are just putting it over on an incompetent European world, and this includes ourselves. . . . Some day we will have an armed conflict with them. . . .

He was slapped down because of his talk about "friendly" Japan in editorials, but he kept on talking. In 1932 he wrote "Will Japan Try to Conquer the United States?" for *Liberty*. Of the Japanese he said:

. . . they are working almost with desperation to make themselves the strongest military power in the world. Their principal aim in doing this is in order to fight the one great white nation on the Pacific Ocean, that is the United States.

In the same article, he recalled the state of American unpreparedness he had seen in Hawaii in 1923:

The last time I was in Honolulu, the officer in command of the army would not speak to the officer commanding the navy. . . . What planning was done was done entirely separately and it was a foolish and dangerous performance.

In other articles in the same year he said that Japan would use surprise tactics, would not declare war, and would aim at Alaska, taking Dutch Harbor in the Aleutians.

He urged American defenses in Alaska, reiterating his belief that "he who holds Alaska will hold the world." But little official attention was paid to him. The Pacific, after all, was the Navy's domain. Whatever had to be done would be done by ships, not by aircraft, except where planes were used to *assist* ships.

In 1932 he had high hopes of a position in which he could work actively for air power in the government. As a result of his repeated testimony certain concessions had been made. The Air Service had been made the Army Air Corps and given more autonomy, or chances to operate on its own. It had been permitted high-ranking officers—even generals such as the enthusiastic air-minded Frank Maxwell Andrews. But most important to Mitchell, a new office had been created in the War Department called Assistant Secretary of Air. When the overthrow of the Republicans came in November, Mitchell believed that he would be given the job. He was, after all, a Democrat by inheritance and faith; he had not fared well in Republican hands.

Naturally [he wrote his friend General Fechet] I will have something to say in the councils of the Democratic Party. As soon as Franklin Roosevelt is relieved from his job as Governor of New York, I am going to take up the whole matter of national defense with him. . . . I have the plans already worked out for these things and when they are made public, they will certainly make some people jump.

What followed was perhaps the greatest disappointment of Mitchell's life. Everywhere during 1933 the rumor ran that the post of Assistant Secretary of Air would surely be given him as compensation for what he had suffered and to bring about real reform in air defense.

If the job is offered you [wrote an old flying friend] for God's sake accept it and take our Air Corps . . . and the Civil Aviation that our broken bodies has made possible out of the hands of politicians. . . .

When the new President came into the White House, the Mitchells were invited to lunch. Mitchell went by himself for several interviews. Mr. Roosevelt was always cordial. Mitchell's visits were reported in the press. It was repeatedly stated that the job was practically in his pocket. Influential members of Congress and advisers to the President recommended his appointment. Yet it was never made.

Several theories about it have been advanced. It is said that Roosevelt was so strongly under the influence of the Navy that he could never bring himself to favor Mitchell. This seems the most likely explanation. The President was air-minded in the end: in 1941 and 1942 the sky became black with planes under his urging; he advocated unity of command in the field and independent strategic air missions in World War II. But in 1933 he was still in love with ships. His desk and the walls of his White House office were covered with pictures and models of them; there were no airplanes there in 1933.

In many ways the ten years following his resignation were the most important of Mitchell's life. In them he consolidated (as the generals say) the ground he had gained. He built the monument to his life which has gained a permanent place in history.

He wrote five books. Two of them were published. Some of the best of them, such as the story of the Alaskan adventure, were never printed. His story about World War I was declined on the ground that there was too much propaganda for a separate air service. In reply to the letter of rejection Mitchell wrote, "This manuscript I wish to be read a hundred years hence, and its present value and sale is entirely a secondary matter to me."

A hundred or so of his articles were published in newspapers and magazines. Here, as in his testimony, there is much repetition. Neither the books nor the articles have literary value. But the body of them represents one of the most persistent campaigns for reform and shows one of the truest visions of a future world that we can find.

And he continued to appear before committees of Congress. He talked about Japan and Germany. He had been greatly impressed by a visit to both Germany and Russia on which he had studied their progress in the air. Despite the handicap of the Versailles treaty the Germans had made alarming strides. He kept talking through the boom and the depression (in which, personally, he suffered), through the peace pacts and the beginning of the League's collapse, and through the coming of Hitler about a second world war.

In the ten years his disciples grew into an army. How familiar their names are since the last war! Apart from "Hap" Arnold and "Tooey" Spaatz, there were Jimmy Doolittle, Lewis Brereton, Delos Emmons, Joe McNarney, and Ira Eaker. And below them were the pilots they commanded and trained and again another vintage of younger pilots who flew the Forts, the Liberators, the Thunderbolts, and the Mustangs and finally the boys in the B-36s and the Sabre jets over Korea. Something was started in those ten years that could not be stopped. Billy Mitchell did not do all of it, or even most of it; the biggest part of all came after the bitter Pacific defeats. Yet, while he lived, he was a kind of catalyst to the whole progress; he kept it moving through the swamps and sloughs and morasses of reaction and backward thought. What he gave was morale.

And then one day, when he was starting out to ride or fish or shoot, he sat down and said, "Betty, I'm tired. Am I growing old?"

He did not understand. He had never in his life been ill. Bed was for sleep. Even when he had broken his bones, he fought against lying down.

The doctor his anxious wife got for him smiled.

"You're fifty-five years old," he said. "You're living as you lived when you were twenty. You ride or hunt or fish or cruise all day and dance all night. You must take it easy."

It was an intolerable thought. The only concession he had made to age so far was to give up flying. Now for a while he tried to do more sedentary things. He wrote his last book, a life of his old protector and friend General Greely. But he could not take it easy for long. The fields, the streams, the stables tempted him too much. It was important to take Lucy and Billy on camping trips. In his last year he taught Billy how to handle a rifle and had a shotgun made for him that would not knock him down. In his last year he made fiery speeches and wrote articles of stern warning. There are no old man's words, no tired words, in them.

If he had spent more time in bed, if he had rested half

the day, he might have lived many years. But he would
not have been Billy Mitchell. He would have "faded away"
as the song says old soldiers do. Such a thing would have
been altogether out of character. The Billy Mitchells of
this world fall with their boots on; they go down in a blaze
of glory.

On January 28, 1936, his heart failed, and his doctor
made him go to the Doctor's Hospital in New York. But he
was there only three weeks. They were his only three weeks
in bed. The power of his mind and will never failed. His
voice did not lose the timbre of youth.

He died on February 20. His Betty, who had been with
him in spirit, in heart, and in deed for thirteen years, was
with him. He left her lonely but not in grief, for she knew
he had died without regret in the midst of life—as if suddenly he had "taken off," up through all overcast, to a
familiar sky.

In the world outside the hospital the new army he had
helped to start never lost a beat in its march. Billy was
still with it: it could not lose him. In the Congress and in
the departments his name was there to conjure with: a
growing chorus repeated it. The rumbling echo of his
words kept filling the Washington corridors, and when the
sieg heils began to be heard in Nuremberg and Berlin and
Vienna, his words ran along the streets, too: "One Department of Defense. A Separate Air Force. Hitler will have
these things. What about us?"

And who can doubt that the spirit of Billy Mitchell
stood scornfully that day in Hawaii when the commander
of the Army and the commander of the Navy still would

not talk to each other about the flying enemy and 3,000 Americans died because a strategic air force dropped bombs on them?

In 1941 Generals Arnold and Eaker wrote:

So far as is known, but three world-known military leaders came away from the first great war with a conviction that a new weapon, vital to modern warfare, had come into existence and that the airplane was that weapon. One of these was our own Brigadier General William Mitchell. Another was Hermann Goering, now Marshal of the Reich, and the third, Admiral W. E. Sims, United States Navy.

General Mitchell came back to a nation which was tired of war, a people which had made a costly sacrifice and wanted to forget it. This was not a fertile soil for his teachings. . . .

Hermann Goering worked under different conditions. . . . His people were smarting under the lash of adversity. Peace treaties closed opportunities to them for great armies and navies. They must turn to another expedient in order to rise from defeat. Goering proposed air power. A new German political school was just emerging and it seized upon his suggestion. The bloody sequel to this story is now being written in the skies above Europe.

Here perhaps is the answer. At the end of World War I, Americans believed that war for us was a thing of the past. It was unthinkable that we could ever be expected to engage in offensive action in the future. The most we might have to do would be to defend our coasts. The Navy was there to do that in its glorious tradition.

The Army and the Navy continued to believe this after the people had begun to doubt. Mitchell's mission was to deepen that doubt . . . to convince the people that the armed forces were wrong. He did not do it all. We have had many teachers: Goering's *Luftwaffe* and Trenchard's Royal Air Force, which knocked it out of the skies over England, as well as the growing body of Mitchell's flying disciples in America. Yet Mitchell's voice cried persistently in the wilderness of American military reaction, and nothing could stop or muffle it until the sound of it was incessant in our ears. After his death its echo seemed like the call of a bugle announcing each catastrophe of the new conflict— in Poland, France, Belgium, Holland, England, and at last in our own Pacific.

"Navies," it said, "oceans and armies are no longer first lines of defense."

16

Long Dreams Come True

THROUGH ALL ITS HISTORY the United States had been protected by oceans. Across the oceans no hostile power had dared venture to attack the rich young nation. Sheltered by the oceans, the American people could enjoy their freedom, conquer their continent, exploit its wealth, and make their country the industrial leader of the world. In security they could build a prosperity which became the envy of civilization. It was necessary, of course, to defend their shores, but with a powerful navy that was easy. The oceans were the basic barriers. Then suddenly, in three hours on a December day in the one hundred and sixty-sixth year of the republic, the oceans "dried up."

On the morning of December 7, 1941, Americans were still talking of "splendid isolation." In the evening of December 7 the word "isolation" had disappeared forever from the American vocabulary. In three hours of flaming horror American concepts of war and peace had completely changed. The old business of breaking off diplomatic relations, of mobilizing the armed forces, of solemnly declaring war—all this was suddenly obsolete. From the moment when that cloud of bombers had come out of the unwatched blue over Pearl Harbor, we must keep looking into the sky for the war which might come in any day or night with less warning than we have from the horizon flashes of an approaching storm. From then on the oceans would be useless for defense; the solid, old "first line" of the Navy's ships was of no more value to us as coastal protection than the famous Maginot folly had been to French land frontiers.

These truths had, of course, been known to many people. To them the drying up, so to speak, of the oceans had not been sudden. The officers and men of the Army Air Corps had for years forgotten the oceans. The Navy's fliers, the skilled young pilots who performed the tricky operations of carrier aircraft, thought of the oceans merely as support for floating bases. It was only the older admirals and the men who had lived long under the beautiful spell of ships who clung sentimentally to the old concept of water as a protection. It was, after all, hard for those who had been brought up on the words "first line of defense" to have to hear that high-sounding phrase changed to "supporting role."

And those who had been in England in the terrible years of 1940 and 1941 and had seen the *Luftwaffe* raining death from the sky while the fabled British navy, which for more than 300 years had protected the island, had been forced to run and hide knew the new score of war. It was the mass of the American people, living so securely through these years of a world on fire, who were shocked and awakened on December 7—they and many of their Senators and Representatives in Washington and, too, many men in swivel chairs in the departments. Probably if the Japanese had measured the extent of the shock which would run like an earthquake through our continent, they would have employed other strategy. The Americans (like the British) were not the sort of people you could safely wake with that particular degree of rudeness. The answer rang across the world in Churchill's contemptuous question, "What kind of people do they think we are?"

And so, as the history books tell us, remembering Pearl Harbor for more than three and a half years, we became totally air-minded, built an air force second to none, operated it strategically and independently over Tokyo, Berlin, and Ploești, carried out decisive air-covered naval operations in the Pacific, sank an immense Japanese tonnage with bombs and aerial torpedoes, and finally dropped an entirely new weapon from B-29s on two Japaneses cities and ended the Japanese war three months after we had helped our allies win the European one. Quite an achievement, on the whole, for a nation whose air power just before the outbreak of war in Europe had been practically negligible! Well, the Fourth-of-July patriots said, there it was, another American miracle. In the end we always came through—no one quite knew how but we always did; we won the wars.

No one quite knew how, it was true, except those who had watched what had gone on behind the scenes.

In the first months of 1942, when there was a great scurrying around in Washington trying to find scapegoats on whom to blame the Pearl Harbor disaster, many people remembered Billy Mitchell. He was remembered in Congress, and the press carried on from there; and before the year was over, it had become the fashion to look wise, wag your finger, and say, "He told you so." The trouble was that most of those who, in these uncertain and bitter months, thought of Billy Mitchell, thought of him in the wrong way.

They remembered accurately enough that he had prophesied the Japanese attack eighteen years before it occurred and that he had repeated the prophecy with urgency just before he died. They remembered that he had prophesied the sinking of battleships from the air twenty years before the *Repulse* and the *Prince of Wales* had gone down and had talked not merely of bombs but of aerial torpedoes. They remembered his words about the Aleutians, about German air power, and about unity of command. They remembered his repeated warnings about the decline of American military air strength. But they then grieved and wrung their hands because all these words had fallen on deaf ears.

Again the wails went up in the chambers of the Capitol. Mitchell was compared to Joan of Arc burned at the stake. One Senator actually stated that he had "died of a broken heart." In the Senate a bill was passed, posthumously restoring Mitchell's rank as brigadier general and then promoting his ghost to major general. The press, eager to support this belated vindication, almost unanimously announced that these honors had actually been conferred—without waiting to see what the House of Representatives would do. (In point of fact no change of rank was ever effected. The "vindication" is part of the Mitchell legend.) Eventually a special medal was issued by Congress which, in spite of what the papers said, was not the Congressional Medal of Honor. It was presented in 1948 to Billy, Jr., in

a dismal apologetic ceremony. This whole mawkish performance (which is still occasionally renewed) is the sort
of thing which Mitchell himself would hold in contempt,
and it is at variance with the truth.

What really happened was that, as his crusade pro-
gressed, fewer and fewer of the ears that listened to Mitchell's words were deaf. Unfortunately, those which until the
end remained deaf were the ears of the "brass." They were
the ears of old men, of reactionaries in both services. They
were turned permanently toward the past. But the ears of
the young men heard Mitchell's call of the future, and their
young minds reflected on it and knew it was so; and you
cannot stop the growth of such a conviction. The fliers
knew because day after day they proved it. They told the
new fliers, and the new fliers told the newer fliers.

Although, in fifteen years following Mitchell's resignation, the bureaus and high echelons of the Army and Navy
did much to fight his crusade and reduced the American air
power almost to impotence, the seeds of his thought had
grown roots so powerful that nothing could destroy them.
Thousands of boys who had never heard his name were
learning to fly, to be at home in the air, to think in air
terms, to study the technics of aircraft, and finally to know
that the air force of the United States had to be independent and coequal with Army and Navy. Designers and
manufacturers of aircraft were constantly revising old plans
and making new ones. All the technics of the air were ad-
vancing day by day, almost hour by hour—not because of
any individual's effort but because the whole level of the
understanding of aviation was rising. The Flying Fortress,
which later became so celebrated in the daylight bombing

of Germany, was already in existence before war broke in Europe and needed only experiment in combat for the bugs to be combed out of it. An organization known as General Headquarters Air Force had trained for independ-ent strategic bombing under the guidance of General An-drews and General Arnold. These things were achieved because the pressure of the airmen was growing year by year until it would become strong enough to overcome all opposition.

It took the immediate threat of war to make the new pattern a reality, to make it a blueprint for action. The point is that the pattern was there. It had been worked out by what Mitchell had called "the fraternity of the air" in spite of all efforts to suppress it. To some extent the very fact of the suppression had worked in its favor as the suppression of the German air force by the Versailles treaty had goaded the men who created the *Luftwaffe* of World War II to work under cover. When General George C. Marshall, who knew the true score and rejected the preju-dices of other generals and admirals, became Chief of Staff, he swept out the cobwebs. He recalled certain officers who had been exiled for their ideas, promoted them to key positions, put an Air Corps officer on the General Staff, induced the President to persuade Congress to make unheard-of appropriations for planes and air force person-nel, and when war came, insisted on unity of command and independent strategic air power. The air generals then, Billy Mitchell's disciples, were ready.

Unhappily, when the war was over, the reactionaries wanted to go back. Unity of command, they said—and that means one boss of Army, Navy, and Air—is all right in the field in a war. It would not do at all in peacetime in Washington! And this air force on its own? It should go back, now that war was ended, to Army and the Navy commands where it could be kept in line.

But then, in 1945, this opposition was crumbling. Only the Navy supported it. The Army had been swung over to unification of the services. Eisenhower, Marshall, Lawton Collins, Omar Bradley—all the generals who had become heroes in the war—wanted a department of defense with Departments of Army, Navy, and Air within it. They wanted one secretary of national defense—a Cabinet officer—with Secretaries of Army, Navy, and Air under him. They wanted to abolish the War Department and the Navy Department as they were then constituted. They wanted, in short, what Billy Mitchell had first advocated twenty-six years before. The Navy held out because the admirals knew that, once the air force had equal standing with it, the Navy would inevitably cease to compose the first line of defense. To give the air force such standing would destroy naval morale—so they said—down to the common seaman.

Two years later Congress passed the National Security Act over the Navy's final protest, and the new National Military Establishment came into being. It was not quite Mitchell's plan. There were a Department of Defense and an independent Air Force at last. But the Navy kept its own aviation, including certain land-based planes. Mitchell's disciples, the men who knew his mind and his desire, wanted something better. But they knew that this was a step and a long one, and for the inspiration which made it possible they thanked him.

What had he done? For what can all Americans thank him?

He told us that there had been a revolution in the world, a revolution started in America on the sands of Kitty Hawk. He told us that until then the history of mankind on earth had been written in two dimensions; that all the future would be written in three. He told us that we could no longer scout danger by leveling our eyes toward the horizons: that we must look up into an element in which armed force could move without the barriers of waves to ensnare its keels or mountains to block its feet. And up there he tried to make men see, not the frail little kitelike craft of his time, but the great winged galleons and even the guided missiles of an unborn era.

He told of the air transport of great cargoes, of armies of men, and of guns. He told these things back in the days of the fabric wings. He told of civil aviation that would revolutionize map making, lead to new geological discoveries, control agricultural pests, speed medical treatment, and make rain over arid regions. He spoke of large commercial transport of passengers and freight on world routes—still back in the days of the first all-metal planes.

If Mitchell had lived to see the new defense, the efficient Air Force, the fulfillment of all the things of which, in his little open Spad, he dreamed, he would not have pointed accusing fingers or laughed in scorn at those who had fought him. There would have been no bitterness or re-crimination, no "I told you so" from Billy Mitchell. "But, of course," he would say today, "we knew—we of the air knew—that all this and more would come. Men who do not fly cannot know these things."

If a man should prophesy that the sun would rise tomor-row, he would not be likely to shout, "I told you so," when it did. To Mitchell air power was precisely as certain. He would have watched every phase, every change, every new technic from jets to space ships with the same intense con-centration that shut out all personal hurts or hates.

There is talk in Congress of monuments, of statues, of static memorials planted in the earth. The monument to Mitchell cannot be so grounded: it moves forever—the silver flash above us, the sky filled with sound.

Sources

IN THE FOLLOWING pages are listed the books, periodicals, manuscripts, and persons which have been consulted in the preparation of this book. References are given to the published portion of Mitchell's diary in case a reader cares to look up this engaging serial story.

CHAPTER 1. The ship bombing is described in detail in William Mitchell's unpublished diary, July 20, 21, 1921, manuscript collection, Library of Congress. Other contemporary accounts are in *Aviation,* July 25, August 1, 8, September 5, 12, 26, 1921; *The New York Times,* July 21, 22, 23, 1921; *New York Tribune,* July 22, 23, 1921; *New York Herald,* July 22, 23, 1921. The author has also interviewed eyewitnesses.

CHAPTER 2. Source material on Alexander Mitchell: John G. Gregory, *History of Milwaukee,* Vol. I, pp. 110, 187; Vol. II, p. 1056; Jerome A. Watrous, *Memoirs of Milwaukee County;* on John Lendrum Mitchell: *ibid.;* on family and boyhood: Eleanor Mercein Kelly, "The Man Who Wouldn't Shut Up," *Collier's,* December 12, 1925; Isaac Don Levine, *Mitchell: Pioneer of Air Power,* chap. 1; letters from Mrs. Martin Fladoes (Harriet Mitchell, sister).

CHAPTER 3. A letter from William Mitchell to his godfather Charles King, April 28, 1930, tells in detail the story of his enlistment in 1898. The material on Mitchell's mother is from Kelly, *op. cit.* In a letter to Major Howard A. Giddings, January 18, 1928, Mitchell tells of the arrest of the drunken soldiers in Washington. The letters are in the manuscript collection, Library of Congress. The Washington Barracks incident is also related in Mitchell, *General Greely,* 1936, pp. 177–181, with the story of the report and Greely's comment. Descriptions of U.S. Army camps: Frederick Funston, *Memories of Two Wars,* 1911. Mitchell's letter to his father quoted at the end of the chapter: Levine, *op. cit.,* p. 28.

CHAPTER 4. Yellow fever in Cuba: William C. Gorgas, *Sanitation in Panama,* 1915, p. 5. Mitchell's experiences in Cuba: *Congressional Record,* Vol. 79, pt. 12, pp. 12688 ff. Philippine insurrection: Walter Millis, *The Martial Spirit,* and Funston, *op. cit.* The latter gives a full account of the capture of Aguinaldo. Mitchell's transfer to Philippines: Levine, *op. cit., passim.* Work in Philippines: Mitchell, *op. cit.,* pp. 190–192.

CHAPTER 5. Sources for all Alaskan material: Annual Report of Chief Signal Officer, U.S. Army, 1902, pp. 3, 4, 7, 8, 10, 52; report of the same officer for 1903, pp. 4, 5, 10; and unpublished book by Mitchell, *The Opening of Alaska,* manuscript collection, Library of Congress.

CHAPTER 6. Mitchell's early experiments with kites and radio: Mitchell, *General Greely.* Statistics on United States air strength and appropriations: AAF, *Official Guide to the Army Air Forces,* 1944, pp. 341, 342; on foreign air expenditures: War Department, Annual Report, 1913, Vol. I, p. 790. Quotation of Mitchell on separation of aviation from Signal Corps: testimony before House Military Affairs Committee, 63:1, "Aeronautics in the Army," 1913, p. 83. Quotation, "The actual flying is a small part. . . .": *ibid.,* p. 81. Quotation, "It has seemed wise . . . not to ask for . . . large appropriation. . . .": *ibid.,* statement of Lindley M. Garrison, Secretary of War.

CHAPTER 7. The main source for this chapter is Mitchell's diary, 1917–1918. Considerable portions of the diary for 1918 were published in a series of articles entitled "Leaves from My War Diary," *Liberty,* March, April, and May, 1928. Dialogue with General Trenchard at the beginning of the chapter: verbatim from the manuscript diary, May, 1917, pp. 21 ff. Description of Pershing's arrival: diary, June, 1917, p. 73. Quotation from Pershing on American air preparedness: John J. Pershing, *My Experiences in the World War,* 1931, Vol. I, p. 27. Meeting with Rickenbacker: diary, July, 1917, p. 96, dialogue constructed from account. Comment on "ridiculous" claims on American airplane production: diary, November, 1917, p. 157. On hunting: diary, September, 1917, p. 127. On boars in road: November, 1917, p. 153. Quotation on General Foulois and aviation officers: diary, November, 1917, p. 150. Pershing's unsent cable: diary, June, 1917, p. 77. For certain material on organization in this and the following chapter, the author is indebted to Brigadier General F. P. Lahm, USA, retired.

CHAPTER 8. World War I flying: Harold E. Hartney, *Up and At 'Em*, 1940; Norman S. Hall, *The Balloon Buster: Frank Luke of Arizona*, 1928; Elmer Haslett, *Luck on the Wing*, 1920; Charles Codman, *Contact*, 1937. Specifications of World War I airplanes: *Jane's All the World's Aircraft*, 1918, 1919. Quotation from Clinton Gilbert: "Mitchell and Air Service," *American Review of Reviews*, April, 1925, p. 376. Exploit of Lieutenants Campbell and Winslow: "Leaves from My War Diary," *Liberty*, March 31, 1928, p. 12. Lufbery incident: *ibid.*, April 7, 1928, p. 34. For the letter about Mitchell's brother John, the author is indebted to Mrs. Martin Fladoes. Material on Patrick: Mason M. Patrick, *The United States in the Air*, 1928, pp. 6, 7, 25. Teamwork of Allied flyers: *Liberty*, May 12, 1928, p. 85. Letter from General Foulois: *Liberty*, April 21, 1928, p. 48.

CHAPTER 9. Fear of air power: Harry A. Toulmin, *Air Service, A.E.F., 1918*, 1927, p. 359. Mitchell's quotation on ignorance of aviation among American troops: *Liberty*, May 5, 1928, pp. 41, 42; p. 42 also gives scatter sheet addressed to Doughboys. Quotation, "It is the first time in history. . . .": diary, September, 1918 (*Liberty*, April 21, 1928, p. 51). Description of preparations for St. Mihiel offensive: Toulmin, *op. cit.*, p. 356. Story of meeting at Pershing's headquarters and of opening of attack: *Liberty*, April 28, 1928, p. 51. Parachute story: unpublished diary; Levine, *op. cit.*, pp. 147–151; *New York American*, May 16, 1926; H. H. Arnold and Ira C. Eaker, *Winged Warfare*, 1941, pp. 55, 56.

CHAPTER 10. Delivery of American airplanes, appropriations, etc.: U.S. Congress, 65:2, Senate Report 555, pp. 1, 2, and U.S. Congress, 66:2, House Report 637, p. 4. "Flaming coffins": U.S. Congress, 68:2, House Select Committee of Inquiry into Operations of the U.S. Air Service (Lampert committee), pp. 1664, 1694–1695, 2155. General Thomas DeWitt Milling's estimate of the old services was given the author in an interview. Quotation, "After the World War, having commanded the organization I did . . . ," is from a letter written by Mitchell to Charles King, April 28, 1930, manuscript collection, Library of Congress. Conference with Navy Board: Levine, *op. cit.*, pp. 169–172; U.S. Congress, 66:3, House Committee on Naval Affairs, Hearing on Sundry Legislation, 1920–1921, p. 746; *Army and Navy Journal,* February 5, 1921, p. 648. Crowell Commission: U.S. Congress, 66:2, House Military Affairs Committee, Hearings before Subcommittee on Aviation, December 4, 1919, February 3, 1920; recommendations of report, pp. 4–6; quotation from speech by Lord Fisher (November 16, 1918), p. 6. Bill authorizing turning over of German ships for bombing test: H. J. Res. 469 (66:3). Discussions of bombing tests: U.S. Congress, 66:3, House Committee on Naval Affiairs, Hearing on Sundry Legislation, pp. 704 ff. Recommendation of Joint Army and Navy Board: *Aviation,* March 14, 1921. Further bombing test information: *Aviation,* June 27, July 4, July 11, 1921. Description of Provisional Air Brigade given to author by General Milling, who commanded it in 1921. Mitchell's divorce: *The New York Times,* November 4, 1922; Levine, *op. cit.,* p. 197.

CHAPTER 11. The parenthetical remarks about the Aviator's Ball are based on news items in *The New York Times,* April 8, 1921. Mitchell's complaints on the Navy's rules for the bombing tests are contained in the report to his superior, Major General Charles T. Menoher, published in *The New York Times,* September 14, 1921. The estimate on the relative cost of the battleship and aircraft is the most conservative of several made by him. It is from U.S. Congress, 66:2, House Appropriations Committee, Hearings on Fortifications Appropriations Bill, p. 366. Navy's retort: report of Joint Army and Navy Board, August 19, 1921, sec. g, par. 24, in *Aviation,* September 5, 1921. Opinions held by Admirals Sims and Fullam on capacities of naval officers: *Aviation,* June 11, 1923, pp. 634 f.; also later testimony of Admiral Sims in Mitchell's trial. For the description of Mitchell's meeting with Miss Miller, his courtship, and their marriage, the author is indebted to Mrs. Thomas Bolling Byrd (Elizabeth Miller Mitchell). The incidents at Selfridge Field are recorded in the papers of General Carl Spaatz, Library of Congress. Mitchell's orders for the honeymoon trip to the Orient, as well as material on the trip itself, are in the Mitchell manuscript collection, Library of Congress. On this, also, the author had the privilege of examining many photograph albums in Mrs. Byrd's possession. All material on the report to General Summerall was taken from correspondence in the manuscript collection, Library of Congress. Mitchell's later testimony on this is recorded in U.S. Congress, 68:2, House Select Committee of Inquiry into Operations of the U.S. Air Services, pp. 2762–2763. Tiger hunt: Mitchell, "Tiger Hunting in India," *National Geographic Magazine*, November, 1924, p. 545. Japan: Mitchell, "Will Japan Try to Conquer the United States?" *Liberty*, June 25, 1932; also testimony before House Select Committee (68:2) p. 294.

CHAPTER 12. Controversial articles on bombing: *Army and Navy Journal*, September 8, 22, 29, 1923. Quotation, "mere cockle-shells" (*New Jersey* and *Virginia*): *ibid.*, September 22, 1923, p. 25. *Ostfriesland* neglect: *ibid.*, September 29, 1923, p. 97. "Broadcasted claim": *ibid.*, editorial on "artificial conditions," September 29, 1923, p. 73. For Mitchell's remarks on Japan see note on Chapter 10 above. Speech at Dayton: *Aviation*, October 20, 1924, pp. 1159, 1160. Material on controversy with Weeks is based on Weeks' testimony before House Select Committee of Inquiry into Operations of the U.S. Air Services, February 28, 1925. Dialogue between Mitchell and Congressman Lea: verbatim from Lampert committee hearings, p. 1683. Letter from Secretary Weeks to President Coolidge, dated March 4, 1925, was introduced in the court-martial trial on December 17, 1925. Quotations from this letter used here were taken from copy in the manuscript collection, Library of Congress. Mitchell's *Winged Defense: The New York Times*, August 29, September 2, 1925.

CHAPTER 13. Political and propaganda use of *Shenandoah* and of West Coast–Hawaii flight: *Aviation*, September 14, 1925, editorial. Itinerary of *Shenandoah: The New York Times*, September 3, 1925. Reports of flight to Honolulu: *The New York Times*, July 13, August 9, 23, 24, 25, 31, September 1, 2, 3, 1925. Log of *Shenandoah: Aviation*, September 14, 1925, p. 312. News of crash: *The New York Times*, September 4, 1925; statement of Secretary Wilbur: *ibid.*; Mitchell's first statement published in full: *The New York Times*, September 6, 1925; Mitchell's first and second statements: *Aviation*, September 14, 1925, pp. 318–

320; Mitchell's justification for his statement is given at length in testimony before the President's Aircraft (Morrow) Board, in the court-martial trial, and in much correspondence after his resignation, notably in a letter to the editor of the Omaha *Bee*, dated March 18, 1926. Opposition: *The New York Times*, editorials, September 7, 11, December 18, 1925; *Congressional Record*, Vol. 67, p. 1357. Admiral Moffatt's statement: *The New York Times*, September 14, 1925; *Aviation*, September 21, 1925, p. 353. Criticism of President's Aircraft Board: *Aviation*, October 5, 1925, pp. 421, 422; October 12, 1925, p. 501. Mitchell's transfer to Washington and arrival: *The New York Times*, September 22, 23, 24, 26, 27, 1925. Birth of Lucy Mitchell: *The New York Times*, August 3, 1925.

CHAPTER 14. Mitchell's costume in Washington: *The New York Times*, September 26, 1925. Quotation on air force defects from testimony before President's Aircraft Board, 1925, Hearings and Report, p. 504. Conservative report: *ibid.*, pp. 1–22. Quotation, "We do not consider. . . .": *ibid.*, p. 14. *The New York Times* editorial quoted here was published on September 11, 1925. Accounts of the court-martial trial: *Aviation*, November 23, December 28, 1925; *Army and Navy Journal*, October 31, November 7, 21, December 12, 19, 1925; *The New York Times*, October 29–December 19, 1925. Admiral Sims's testimony: *Army and Navy Journal*, November 21, 1925, p. 295. Mitchell's final statement: *Aviation*, December 28, 1925. Prosecutor's statement: *The New York Times*, December 19, 1925.

CHAPTER 15. Quotation from Clinton Gilbert: "Mitchell in the Air Service," *American Review of Reviews*, April, 1925, pp. 377, 378. Letter to John Cudahy, dated November 30, 1930, and that to Arthur Brisbane, December 1, 1931, are in the manuscript collection, Library of Congress. Quotations from "Will Japan Try to Conquer the United States?": *Liberty*, June 25, 1932, pp. 6, 10. The statement on Alaska was made to the House Committee on Military Affairs in February, 1934. Letter to James Fechet, November 23, 1932: manuscript collection, Library of Congress. Quotation on Mitchell, Goering, and Sims: H. H. Arnold and Ira C. Eaker, *op. cit.*, 1941, p. 2. Much of the material in this chapter is based on personal interviews with Mitchell's family and friends.

CHAPTER 16. Attempts at posthumous restoration of Mitchell's rank: *Congressional Record*, Vol. 92, p. 9259. S. J. Res. 109, 77:2, passed Senate first time January 12, 1942. Presentation of medal to William Mitchell, Jr.: United Press dispatch, "Air Force Vindicates Gen. Billy Mitchell," March 27, 1948. Army and Navy attitudes on unification: U.S. Congress, 80:1, Senate Armed Services Committee, "National Defence Establishment."

Index

70-ꝗ